Warm Water

THE LAST ACT OF COMPASSION

---※---

A Collection of Stories by a Hospice Nurse

PEPPER CAPPUCCIO

ISBN 978-1-0980-7042-7 (paperback)
ISBN 978-1-0980-7043-4 (digital)

Copyright © 2020 by Pepper Cappuccio

All rights reserved. No part of this publication may be reproduced, distributed, or transmitted in any form or by any means, including photocopying, recording, or other electronic or mechanical methods without the prior written permission of the publisher. For permission requests, solicit the publisher via the address below.

Christian Faith Publishing, Inc.
832 Park Avenue
Meadville, PA 16335
www.christianfaithpublishing.com

Printed in the United States of America

In loving memory of my mother.
Joanne Frances Cappuccio.
A teacher, mentor, confidante and friend.

I wish to thank my nephew, PJ Amendolia for his help and expertise in writing this book.

"What we do for ourselves dies with us. What we do for others and the world remains and is immortal".
Albert Pine.

PREFACE

Hospice nurses have the unique opportunity to care for patients who have been diagnosed with a terminal disease and are now living at home. We, as the nurse, care for these patients. We are afforded much more time to spend one-on-one moments with these patients in their personal environment. During that time, we develop rapport with both the patients and their families and caregivers. It can be a very emotional experience. While we are providing the support and reassurance necessary for them during this unimaginable time, we often experience our own catharsis. Not all people experience the dying process in the same way. Some are completely devastated. Some are in denial. Others are private and don't wish to share their feelings, while others are eager to share every detail. Our job as a hospice nurse is to offer emotional support to these families and loved ones and to facilitate the healing process of grief. Each patient and family follows their faith as a resource for a successful recovery from this spiritual event.

Sometimes simply listening attentively can make a world of difference.

This collection of personal experiences illustrates the gift of healing through grief and further demonstrates the power of interacting with families and loved ones as it not only heals the people affected by the recent loss but also has a profound effect on the hospice nurse.

ONE

The Alcoholic

A call came in from the dispatcher: "Patient very agitated and combative towards family, visit needed immediately."

I gathered my nurse bag and traveled to the patient's home, twenty miles north of where I live.

It was very cold, the temperature was near zero, and the roads were iced over. I could drive at only twenty-five miles an hour in my new Ford Fusion. The highway was deserted, as it usually is this time at night in January. The past week was very busy for me. New Year's Eve and, of course, celebrating my nephew's twenty-first birthday. Despite feeling a little worn out, I must do my job. Attend to the dying and the dead.

After fifty minutes of driving, I turned down Cherry Street to house number 211. The only light on was the small yellow light at the far end of the porch. As it flickered in the wind, I was very careful as I made my way to the front door.

I was met at the door by the patient's daughter, Lisa. She was disheveled and distraught. The ordeal of caring for her father was obviously having a devastating effect on her.

"Hello," I said. "I'm Pepper, the hospice nurse."

Lisa replied, "I am so relieved you are here. My father is doing much worse. Can you please help him?"

"I will do everything I can," I offered as reassurance.

"Daddy has not slept for more than forty-eight hours, and now, he is acting very mean. He is saying things that don't make sense. Please help him."

Whenever I arrive at the patient's home, the caregivers are usually exhausted and having difficulty coping with the progression of the patient's disease and the worsening condition of their loved one. It becomes my job to alleviate the emergent problem at hand and to offer the support and reassurance needed by the families in this time of need.

Upon entering the home, I could hear the patient, Robert, yelling at his daughter, "Let me get out of this bed. I need to get to the garage. My car is ready for the flight. I must get in now so I can meet the others."

As I looked around, I could see the house looked like it hadn't been cleaned in weeks. The smell of dirty dishes wafted from the kitchen sink. The room was cluttered with extra blankets, medical supplies, and an abundance of half-full trash bags that no one had removed from the room.

Robert was having hallucinations more regularly now. Lisa pleaded with me to help make her father more comfortable and calm.

Robert's ex-wife, Irene, was observing from across the room.

He was on hospice due to liver failure. He had been an alcoholic for most of his adult life. He was often fired from his job for drunkenness and disorderly conduct. He barely provided for his family and was absent in his daughter's life.

Irene agreed to allow Robert to stay with them during his final days.

On assessment, Robert was very uncomfortable. He was in severe pain, short of breath, and extremely restless. Nothing so far was helping to alleviate his symptoms.

Multiple doses of morphine and Haldol were administered to treat Robert's symptoms. He was experiencing terminal agitation, a syndrome that may occur at the end of life. Patients may exhibit physical, emotional, or spiritual restlessness as death nears.

A short time after the medications were administered, Robert became calmer.

Suddenly, I heard a loud rumbling in his abdomen. Instinctively, I moved to his side just as he expelled a large amount of black-tarry liquid from his mouth.

Projectile vomiting!

Nursing school prepped me with some pretty nasty experiences, but this scene was one of the worst I'd ever seen.

Robert became very quiet after that episode. His breathing became very shallow, and his eyes were glazed over. Robert then looked into my eyes. I remember feeling that he was somehow asking permission to do the thing he was supposed to do.

Pass away.

Cross over.

Begin that last journey, or perhaps the beginning of a new journey altogether.

Or as often is the case at the very end of life, Robert was silently asking me to do the thing that I was in his home to do. He needed comfort, as he would leave this earth. I did that for him. I held his hand and told him, "It's all right. You can be at peace now."

In just a few moments, as Robert was still looking into my eyes, he took his last breath and became still.

Silence fell across the room and through the entire home. The only sound one could hear was a low ticking of a wall clock whose time was off by around thirty minutes.

As I continued looking down at my now-deceased patient, I believe I had a sense that his spirit was leaving this battered body and ascending upward to the heavens. The patient's daughter was stunned by the sudden relaxation of her father's body, the way he was now silent and not wrenching and hollering out in pain and frustration from his discomfort. The way he now seemed to be cooperating with the encouragement from me, his nurse, to try to calm down and be at peace.

She wiped a tear from her left cheek and pleaded to me, "Is he going to be all right now?"

I was speechless at first, and then I too welled up with tears. I had to tell this innocent child of sixteen years that her father, whom she obviously loved very much, was not going to be all right.

He had in fact passed away.

Died.

Gone to heaven.

How else could I explain it to this child? The truth was, he was at peace now. His suffering had ended. No more severe pain or struggling to breathe. No more feeling guilty over his absence from this child's young years from his alcoholism.

Just as I was about to cross the "hospice line" and become overly emotional, the patient's wife exclaimed, "Don't feel bad. He was a worthless piece of garbage who did nothing for his family."

I was taken aback by this insensitive verbal assault about a man that had just passed away in violent fashion. It seemed so harsh, even coming from an ex-wife.

Before I could respond, she said, "But I guess I will miss him. I loved him, you know."

My only reply was, "I am so sorry for your loss."

I have been a hospice nurse for several years and have seen a tremendous amount of suffering from both patients and their families. I have been fortunate a handful of times to be with a patient at precisely the moment they left this earth. Other times, I would attend to a patient after they had passed away. I would prepare the patient for their journey to a funeral home and then attend to the spiritual needs of the patient's loved ones. The experiences have been eye-opening and humbling. They help me to place my own life's experience in a different perspective.

Those little things we think are important to us become nonconsequential when you witness someone experiencing their impending mortality. There are lessons to be learned from the dying patient. Lessons you would think we should already know. Lessons perhaps taught by our religious affiliations or lessons passed on by our parents.

I can sometimes be surprised by the statements made by the loved ones of the patient. Some are expected; some are not.

After the family accepted that Robert was now gone, I began my duties for the deceased patient.

Time of death: 11:42 p.m.

I requested that Irene bring me some warm water to bathe Robert.

Although the patient has passed away, using warm water to bathe them is a way of continuing the compassionate care offered by hospice workers and conveys respect for the human who has left this world for another. Most loved ones are very appreciative of this gesture and usually open up about their relationship with the patient.

I began removing Robert's clothes. He was still dressed in jeans and overalls. He insisted on keeping on his usual attire. In his mind, wearing pajamas would be a sign of defeat, giving in to the process. I needed to change all the bed linens after that explosive mess at the last minute. I bathed Robert and placed clean clothes on him that were provided by Lisa. I called the funeral home and requested that he be picked up at the home and taken into their care.

Once the patient is taken care of, I turn my attention to the loved ones. They are the ones who are experiencing loss now.

They need our attention now.

They have been caring for the patient around the clock.

Irene was very open and talked about Robert and the struggles they had as a result of his drinking.

"We met at a bar in Atlantic City. We drank our asses off that night. I had no idea Robert would drink that much alcohol all the time. We had such high hopes for the future. Robert wanted to finish college and earn a degree in economics. I guess the pressure of school, and marriage, and me becoming pregnant before we were married contributed to the 'problem.'"

She did in fact love him very much, and even in her blatant resentment toward him prior, she was heartbroken.

She stated, "Things don't always work out the way you planned." She needed to forgive her husband for his "shortcomings." Being there for him during his last days was something she felt she must do. If she had truly thought he was garbage, she would not have been there for him. Love, even in this subtle and complex form, was still present for her deceased husband.

TWO

Lung Cancer

Jane had been a heavy smoker for thirty-five years. She was now fifty-five years old and was recently diagnosed with stage IV lung cancer. She grew up around smokers her whole life. Her mother died of breast cancer at forty, and her father died in a car accident when Jane was just twelve. Jane ignored her physician's advice of quitting smoking.

Dispatcher call: "Patient unable to catch her breath. Caregiver instructed to administer morphine, 10 mg, under her tongue. Visit requested."

I started driving to attend to the patient's needs. As I entered the highway, I remembered how difficult it was for me to stop smoking cigarettes. I, along with both my parents and two female siblings, smoked like chimneys all the time. We never did much of anything without stopping to take a drag, or many drags. It was just something most of my family, as well as several families, did casually.

Smoke tobacco.

I turned on the radio and found a favorite Barry Manilow song playing. "Can't Smile without You." The song transported me back to a time when several loved ones who had passed on as a result of smoking cigarettes were still with us. My mother, my favorite aunt, and a great friend were the first to pop into my head. I thought how, if these people were able to stop that nasty addiction, they might still be with us today, enjoying life.

As a nurse, one shall not and will not judge anyone, especially in death.

I arrived on Jane's street rather quickly. She lived in a two-story brick home. Her house was on the corner with a wraparound driveway. The grass on the front lawn was overgrown, and there was paper litter everywhere. Old candy wrappers, used cigarette butts, and empty soda cans. I walked up to the front door and rang the doorbell. Richard, Jane's husband, answered the door immediately.

"Hi, I'm Pepper, the hospice nurse."

"Thank God," Richard replied. "Please come in."

As I entered the home, the stench of nicotine was overwhelming, like the ashtray had never been emptied. The window drapes, once a crisp white fabric, were now stained yellow with nicotine. The carpet leading to the bedroom was worn and stained. Wheelchair marks embedded in the carpet marked a trail straight to Jane. I introduced myself to Jane.

It was all she could do to just wave her right hand to motion me inside her bedroom and have a seat.

Jane was too exhausted to speak. On assessment, Jane was struggling to breathe. Her blood pressure was 188/100, her heart rate was 120, and her respirations were 32 breaths per minute.

Immediately, Jane was administered more morphine, 20 milligrams, sublingual, and Ativan, 1 milligram, by mouth. Her oxygen was increased to 3 liters per minute.

With a hoarse voice, Jane asked, "Is this the end?"

I immediately administered an additional large dose of morphine, along with Ativan. She seemed to have some relief; however, it was clear she was very concerned about this latest episode of difficult breathing.

Richard began telling me how Jane was declining the past two days. She was staying in bed all the time, eating very little, and coughing constantly. Her oxygen and breathing treatments were not very helpful.

I held Jane's hand in an attempt to console her.

Richard was very silent as his eyes welled up with tears. He had a sense, as did Jane, that her time was running short.

While Ativan was helping Jane's anxiety, her breathing was still difficult. Her respirations were still in the high 20s. I administered an additional dose of 20 milligrams of morphine. This dose did slow the rapid breathing. In fact, Jane was now so sedated that her breaths decreased to 8 per minute. She was very calm, and as with other patients, Jane looked into my eyes and very quietly drifted off.

Breathing ceased.

Jane was gone.

Time of death: 5:15 p.m.

Richard sat next to his beloved wife and began sobbing.

I placed my hand on Richard's shoulder and offered my condolences. He answered by telling me about his first date with Jane. They were at a country square dance. Richard was a smoker back then as well. After a few months, they were in love. Soon, they married and had been together for twenty-two years. Richard had a heart attack five years ago and quit smoking. He stated that he pleaded with Jane to quit as well. Try as she might, Jane had no success.

Now she was gone.

I asked Richard for a basin of warm water and went about the ritual of preparing Jane for the funeral home.

The only piece of clothing Jane was wearing was a stained nightgown that Richard clumsily placed on her after he changed her. Jane was incontinent of urine and was going frequently. Richard did the best he could. I took the nightgown off and gave Jane a complete bath and then placed a new clean gown. Once finished, I turned my attention to the love of Jane's life.

"What can I do for you?" I asked Richard.

Richard took a deep breath and said, "All of the nurses and home health aides who cared for Jane were so wonderful. I could never have cared for her as much as they did. Because they did all that work for me, I was able to spend so much quality time with Jane. Jane told me she had such guilt and shame from continuing to smoke cigarettes. She knew, someday, she would regret that nasty habit."

Richard continued, "I hold no resentment for her choices. I just wish I could have Jane for a little while longer."

I asked Richard how he and Jane had met.

Richard said he first met Jane while she was working as a waitress in a diner near Philadelphia. He had stopped in for a quick lunch and sat at the counter, and Jane walked up to him with a fresh pot of coffee in one hand and a "great big smile." Richard, who had just gone through a bitter divorce from his first wife, Susan, was absolutely smitten.

He asked her to attend a square dance on Friday night.

It was love at first sight!

THREE

Is He Gone?

I was still on orientation for my new job, and I was sent to a patient's home for a pronouncement. There is a certain protocol followed for each pronouncement. You check the patient for breathing and heart rate. If neither are present, the patient has passed.

Dispatcher call: "Patient may have passed away. Son requesting urgent visit."

I left the house immediately and notified my coworker that I will probably arrive at the patient's home before her. I stated that I will wait outside until she arrives.

Anxiety gripped me as I contemplated how I might react to my first pronouncement. I struggled with coming to terms with this, but I had to remember how important palliative care is for suffering patients. I turned on the radio, and the music playing was not what I was in the mood for. I popped in a CD of one of my favorites, Dionne Warwick. The song "After You" began to play. I understand it is a song about a breakup between lovers; however, it seemed to be more appropriate for someone who has just lost a loved one through death.

The traffic was very heavy during the rush hour. I changed lanes several times to ensure my trip would be as speedy as possible. I also probably cursed out a couple of people on my way in because driving in New Jersey does not come without challenges. I shouldn't make the family wait too long for our arrival. The patient lived in an over-fifty retirement community with his wife, Linda.

As I drove in the driveway of Anthony's house, his son, William, came rushing out the front door to rush me inside. He was not sure if his father had passed away or not. I quickly got out of my car, ran inside, and began assessing the patient. By this time, Linda and several other people were gathered on a large couch behind me, waiting for the "word" about Anthony.

There were a few lights on in the home. I could smell old kitty litter and spotted two oversized elderly cats perched on a worn easy chair. I presume this was where Anthony might have sat before he became bedbound. The smell of stale coffee permeated the air.

As I approached Anthony, I could see he was very stiff. Rigor mortis had already begun. The patient was stiff: limbs unmovable.

It was very obvious Anthony was gone.

I went through the steps. Listened for the breaths and for the beating of the heart.

There was no doubt that my patient had passed away.

Time of death: 6:40 p.m.

I turned around and very quietly told his wife, "I am so sorry for your loss."

Without any hesitation, Linda stood up and yelled, "Anthony! Anthony! Anthony!" She seemed to be shocked that he had died. She went to the bedside and began shaking the bed rails, trying to shake Anthony awake. She then looked at me and asked again, "Are you sure he died?"

Again, time to console the loved one.

I sat down with Linda and offered more emotional support. Asked her how long she and Anthony had been together. She told me this was her second marriage and his third. They were married just one year ago when he was diagnosed with a brain tumor. She went through all the signs and symptoms with me as if I were a student of medicine. She told me how they recommended extensive treatment, including chemotherapy and radiation. How he was so sick from that treatment. I stayed and listened for as long as she needed.

When she was finished, I requested the warm water to wash her late husband.

Once Anthony was bathed, dressed, and ready to go, I asked if there was anything Linda would like me to do.

She said, "Please stay until our priest arrives to bless Anthony."

"No problem. It would be an honor," was my reply. "Tell me more about Anthony as we wait."

Linda and Anthony were devout Catholics. Although they were each married multiple times prior to their union, they had remarkably strong faith and continued to go to church every Sunday together as if they were newlyweds.

As it turned out, Anthony was born in Nicastro, Italy, a small town in the province of Catanzaro, in the Calabria region of Southern Italy. Anthony and his parents moved here when he was six years old. He could speak fluent Italian as well as English.

Linda is Irish. Her parents were natives of Belfast. She grew up very poor and married her first husband because she became pregnant shortly after they had met. Linda and her first husband had only one child named Michael.

William, the one that answered the door upon my arrival, was Anthony's son from his second marriage.

Linda and I talked for over an hour before Father Mark and the mortician arrived. She was very grateful that I stayed with her during that time.

During that short time, several of Anthony's relatives had arrived to join those already present. They each had offerings of food. Some dishes were prepared, and some needed to be prepared in the home.

Soon the home was filled with the scent of fresh-cooked garlic and other herbs, like basil, oregano, onions, and so on. The smells of the newly started Italian gravy began to permeate the kitchen, and I suddenly felt transported back to my grandmother's house many years ago.

As a child, every adult smoked cigarettes in the home. Basically, that was the primary scent every day. When we would visit my grandmother, however, I would be met with the wonderful smells of Italian cooking as I entered the home.

Of course, it wasn't until later in life, after quitting the smoking habit, that I could truly appreciate the joys of being able to smell and be reminded of the efforts made by our elders to make life memorable.

I told Linda that sharing her stories with me about Anthony was very interesting. They transported me back in time.

Linda said, "You made me feel a little better on this sad day."

Grazie!

FOUR

Am I Sure?

As a hospice nurse, I have always had a terrible fear of pronouncing a patient who might not be completely "gone."

Dispatcher call: "Patient has passed away. Need a visit now."

I drove to the home of Elizabeth Donaldson, a ninety-four-year-old retired schoolteacher who lived on the lake in a secluded retirement village in southern New Jersey.

The weather was warm and humid. I cranked up the air-conditioning in the car, turned on the radio, and began my journey. The address was not too far from my house.

I turned onto Third Street and parked in front of number 203. The house was a two-story Colonial built in the mid-1930s. The property was well maintained. Grass neatly groomed, sidewalks swept clean, and multiple glass windows glistening in the sun.

I walked up the brick stairs to the porch and used the engraved door knocker to alert the caregiver that I had arrived.

As the door opened, a handsome, well-groomed man who was neatly dressed in Alfani slacks and a pullover top designed by Tasso Elba met me.

I introduced myself. "Hi, I'm Pepper, the hospice nurse."

"Good Afternoon, I am Jason Donaldson. I am Elizabeth's son."

As I entered the home, I passed through the patient's library. I quickly noticed the many collections of books from various authors, many of whom I have read and enjoyed in the past. Sidney Sheldon, Mary Higgins Clark, John Grisham, and James Patterson, to name a few. Elizabeth also had original copies of *Gone with the Wind* and *The Red Badge of Courage*. I continued through the library and into the den, where her son, Jason, had set up a hospital bed and oxygen. Elizabeth had been suffering from congestive heart failure and recently became tired, weak, and dependent on continuous oxygen to breathe.

Elizabeth had always been a person who prided herself with cleanliness. The home was filled with pleasing scents. The first smell to envelope my senses was that of Pine-Sol. Her son must have freshened the bathrooms prior to my arrival. Lemon Pledge had soaked into the wood shelves of the bookcases in the library.

Next, as I came closer to Elizabeth's room, I could make out the scents of an older woman's perfume tray. It reminded me of my mother's scents in her bedroom. As a little kid, I would play in her bedroom and sample the pleasant fragrances around my neck. Her favorite was Chanel N°5.

I went through the necessary protocol, checked her breathing, and listened for a heartbeat.

Elizabeth was dead.

Passed away.

Gone to heaven.

Time of death: 4:35 p.m.

I announced to Jason that I was very sorry for his loss. He asked me to be very sure she was dead, stating, "She still feels warm." It takes some time for the body to cool after one has passed away, so while the body was not cold, I assured him that his mother had passed away. She had no pulse.

I asked Jason for a basin of warm water, which he quickly brought to me, and I began the task of preparing the patient for her trip to the funeral home.

I started by removing Elizabeth's laced pajama top. As I leaned in to bring the top over her head, I pushed down on her left shoulder.

Then it happened. A moan escaped from Elizabeth's mouth! I was terrified!

I attempted to remove the top again, and again, a moan. Could I have been wrong? Was this my worst fear realized?

At that moment, Jason entered the room and heard the most recent moan and began to scream with excitement:

"Mom is still alive!"

I looked at him and immediately said, "No, I'm sorry Mom has passed. I'm not sure why she is making sounds. Please allow me to finish."

Jason turned and left the room. I then called the physician on call to report my findings. She explained that this could happen sometimes to patients who have had a high fever just before death. Gases can build up inside the body, and when the body is moved, it can moan or groan.

Of course, if the body starts to speak, then they may not be dead after all. Once I explained all this to Jason, he seemed convinced and called the funeral home.

As we waited for the funeral home workers to arrive, Jason was interested in telling me about his life as Elizabeth's son. He began by telling me Elizabeth adopted him after both his parents died in a plane crash more than forty years ago. The plane was traveling from New Jersey to Boston during a historic snowstorm. The plane crashed as it was trying to land on an ice-covered runway.

Jason continued on, "Mom was a very strong woman. She was married for a very brief time, got a divorce, and never abandoned the dream of being a mother. I never felt insecure or unloved. She was the best."

Jason brought me the basin of warm water as requested. I finished the preparation and offered more condolences to Jason. He was very appreciative and stated he wished to make a donation to our hospice as a thank-you.

Elizabeth made me second-guess my pronouncement skills, but only for a minute.

FIVE

May I Have Some Wine?

When visiting patients at night or on the weekend, I seldom become emotionally attached. At least, not in the same way as the patient's primary nurse. Often, the visit may be the very first time that I meet the patient and their loved ones. There was one special patient whom I needed to visit each Saturday and Sunday to check on her Dilaudid infusion. Sometimes patients with severe, difficult-to-manage pain are placed on an IV infusion to allow for the patient and family to administer extra doses without having to wait for the nurse to travel each time.

Diane, a fifty-nine-year-old woman with ovarian cancer, lived in a shore town in New Jersey. Diane was one exception to the rule or norm of not getting attached to patients I see infrequently or during the weekends.

Living with Diane were her husband, Joe, and their son, Joe Jr. Every Saturday and Sunday, for about six months, I would travel the Atlantic City Expressway to her home to check on her infusion. Her home was directly on the waterfront, and her husband had a nice-sized boat docked just outside. Each time I entered the home,

I was amazed at how beautiful the foyer and entranceway looked. The gray-and-white swirled marble floors and the crystal chandelier hanging midway from the cathedral ceiling. I remember the soft music echoing throughout the house as Diane was sitting in her favorite recliner looking out at the bay.

Today was a particularly humid day. The air was filled with the smell of salt and seaweed. Diane had an unobstructed view of the mainland. The sky was a clear blue sky with no clouds to be seen. The ocean was light-emerald green with an unusual calmness for this time of year.

Inside, the smell of fresh ground coffee permeated the kitchen as I walked by to get nearer to Diane.

"Good morning, Pepper!" she cheerfully exclaimed as I came into her view.

"Good morning, Diane. How are you feeling today?"

"My pain is much better now that we have increased the frequency and dose amount. Joe just went for a shopping trip to the grocery store. I always love to see my weekend nurse."

"Thank you. May I take your vital signs now?"

"Sure."

Diane was diagnosed less than two years ago with stage IV ovarian cancer. She started having severe abdominal pain and bleeding. By the time the doctors figured out what the cause was, it was too late. Diane still went through a round of chemotherapy and radiation without success. Soon after that, Diane was admitted to hospice and consequently started on the infusion for her pain management.

My visits continued for six months or so. Each time, Diane was pleasant and attempted to mask the reality of what was happening to her. She was becoming weaker, her appetite was decreasing, and she was beginning to look more and more like a cancer patient who was going to die. I began to notice how her memory was fading, and she was unable to walk.

One warm Sunday morning in May, I made my visit to Diane. I immediately sensed she had something on her mind.

"Hello, Diane."

"Hello, Pepper."

"How are you feeling today?" I dreaded asking that question. We both knew what the real answer was.

"I'm not doing too well today. I feel worse than ever," she said. The unending pain was etched on her face.

"Tell me what's wrong," I asked.

"My pain is not quite under control, and I can't seem to keep anything down."

"All right, let me call the physician and get new orders to increase the Dilaudid."

"Thank you. I also want to ask you something."

"Sure, what is it?"

"Well, since this whole cancer thing started, I have not drunk any wine or cocktails, thinking it might hurt me somehow. Do you think it would be all right?"

"Of course it is all right. Where is the wine?"

"It's in the wine rack next to the refrigerator. I love Riesling. Joe took me to Germany on our honeymoon and introduced me to many delicious wines."

"Riesling is one of my favorites as well," I said.

Without hesitation, I opened the bottle and poured Diane a glass of her favorite wine. I also poured a tiny bit in my glass (just to be polite, of course).

Diane raised her glass and said, "To a long road that will come to an end soon."

As she sipped her wine, Diane started talking about her life with Joe and how lucky it was that they met and married. She talked about the love she had for her only child, Joe Jr. Sometimes Joe Jr. would be present for the visits. He was always very polite, but not much of a talker. It seemed that every time I arrived to tend to his mother, Joe Jr. would leave the home.

Diane's husband, on the other hand, could talk for hours. He would talk about his boat, the many excursions he and Diane had taken on that boat, and how he loved to fish.

All of this, while avoiding the inevitable.

Diane started feeling sleepy after drinking half her glass and asked me to place the glass on her side table.

Soon, Diane was asleep, appearing very comfortable.

I finished my visit and returned to my home.

Dispatcher call: "Patient passed away. Husband requesting visit to pronounce."

I was barely home when the return call came in.

I began my trip back to Diane.

When I arrived, Joe met me at the door. He had been crying.

"Come right in," Joe said.

The music was off. The house was silent. It felt like no one was there.

Diane was silent.

Time of death: 3:15 p.m.

After confirming her passing, I turned to Joe and offered my condolences.

"Joe, I am so sorry for your loss."

"Thank you, Pepper. I was here for her last breaths. She wanted me to say thank you to you. She said you made her last day very special."

I could not hide my emotion this time. I began to cry. Joe was now consoling me. I somehow became attached to this beautiful person. That is something that is unavoidable sometimes. I'm not ashamed or embarrassed. I am grateful for having met this woman and her husband. I am still thankful I had the opportunity to grant her that wish of one last glass of wine.

I filled her basin with warm water and started her last bath.

Au revoir, I thought to myself, wishing Diane the finest wines in a more peaceful place.

SIX

Too Young to Leave

There cannot be any loss greater than that of a child, your own flesh and blood.

Laura was a very energetic sixteen-year-old girl who was living her life like any other girl that age. Going to school, playing with her friends, and planning her future after high school. Laura was an average student academically. She did enjoy playing field hockey and softball for her high school. She also enjoyed her family, especially her two younger brothers, Luke and Shawn.

One cool autumn afternoon, Laura was practicing hockey with her teammates on the home field when, suddenly, she became very winded and had a hard time breathing.

The coach administered oxygen from the sideline equipment to help stabilize his player. Laura recovered nicely. The next day, her father, Carl, took her to their primary care physician for assessment. The physician was concerned after his evaluation and ordered several diagnostic tests: a chest X-ray, electrocardiogram, and blood tests.

Some tests were abnormal, so a Heart Catheterization was ordered. The physician called Carl once the results were in. Laura had been diagnosed with leukemia. Usually, this disease can be treated successfully in people less than twenty years of age. Unfortunately,

Laura had also developed advanced lung cancer, stage IV. Treatment options were limited. Despite the lack of choices, she did start chemotherapy and radiation.

The cancer did not respond to treatment. It was any parent's worst nightmare coming true.

In less than three months, Laura was admitted to hospice for management of her symptoms and end-of-life care.

Caring for a younger patient presents many challenges. The patient is entitled to their wishes. The patient often brings up the subject of death. The emotional and spiritual support offered to the young patient is very important. The complicated and upsetting family dynamics also play a role. The hospice team collaborated with psychologists and other specialists with background in treating children who were dying.

Dispatcher call: "Patient is in respiratory distress. Father instructed to administer morphine and Ativan as directed."

Prior to my departure from home, I looked up the case file for Laura. I was somewhat anxious at her young age. I didn't know what to expect, and although I don't have children of my own, the circumstances of this case made the job much more difficult.

I was uneasy about this visit.

I entered the highway. Another frigid night. Roads were clear, and no ice covering the shoulders as is usually the case this time of year. The patient lived in a small rural town in southern New Jersey, just a few miles north of the Delaware Memorial Bridge. My usual radio station played my favorite oldies. Tonight there was a block of music from Michael Jackson. "Billie Jean," "Black or White," and "You Are Not Alone." That last song would have special meaning in a short while. As I turned down Carlisle Street, I became more anxious, not knowing what to expect.

I parked the car and rang the doorbell.

After what seemed like an eternity, Carl answered the door.

"Hi, my name is Pepper. I'm the hospice nurse."

Carl said, "Hello, come in please. I'm afraid you are too late."

Carl led me back to Laura's bedroom. Along the way, I noticed the living room walls were covered with large portraits of Carl's three children. They were arranged in no particular order. All three children looked like Carl. I also noticed there were no portraits of a mother, a wife, a female presence.

Once there, I began the final assessment.

Time of death: 8:05 p.m.

I looked at Carl and offered condolences and support.

He was inconsolable. It is perhaps the hardest and most unnatural thing for any parent to have to go through.

Carl wept loudly and asked, "Why?" Until this moment, I would usually offer my support to the children of the patient, not the other way around.

What could I possibly say to this man? What words could ease his pain? Nothing I could say would ever fix or heal this new void in his life.

I decided I would let Carl vent to me if he needed to do so. I asked who the boys were in the portraits.

"They are my sons, Joe and Robert. They are staying with my sister in Philadelphia."

"Are you here alone?" I asked.

"Yes. My wife died three years ago. I don't know if she could have taken this."

"Will you be alone tonight?"

"No. My wife promised me on her deathbed. You will never be alone. It is that promise that will comfort me tonight. My wife is gone and now, my daughter is gone, but I am not alone," Carl said, as the tears continued to trickle down his exhausted face.

I looked around the room and spotted a basin for the warm water.

Carl said, "Please let me bathe my daughter with you. I will never be able to touch her again after tonight."

Of course I allowed him to help me. I had never found this task to be as challenging as it was with Laura. I contacted the funeral director of his choice.

I could not imagine he would ever come to terms with the tragedy that unfolded.

I felt very much alone as I drove home.

My radio was silent.

SEVEN

An Artist's Gift

One of the most difficult hospice cases I endured was that of a seventeen-year-old young man named Louis. Louis was diagnosed with hepatocellular carcinoma at age fifteen. This is a rare type of malignant cancerous tumor that forms in the cells and tissues of the liver. Symptoms include abdominal pain, nausea, vomiting, weight loss, and jaundice (a yellowing of the skin or eyes). Louis went through the recommended treatments, including surgical removal of the tumor and chemotherapy. At first, the treatments were successful in slowing the progression of the disease. After about one year of remission, the cancer returned and had now metastasized to his bowel. In January, right after the holidays, Louis was admitted to hospice for pain management.

I was called out to the home frequently for pain issues and nausea. Each time I went to the home, Louis's dad, James, was present and able to provide me the information needed during the assessment, and I was able to offer additional support to his son.

Louis's mom, Janice, was always in a different room, unable to be at the bedside during these frequent episodes of pain and nausea. I thought this was a little strange for her to seem physically and emotionally absent during these visits, but I figured her grief was being manifested differently than her husband's. The home was very close to the Walt Whitman Bridge, near Camden, New Jersey. A three-bedroom rancher with an in-ground pool in the backyard. James would later tell me that Louis loved the pool and was a champion swimmer. He had come in first or second in virtually every competition. He had even applied for a scholarship to the University of California, Berkeley. Unfortunately, that ambition of the future was never going to happen now.

Dispatcher call: "Patient minimally responsive. Visit requested."

I dreaded this call for some time. Similar to James and Janice, I couldn't imagine a parent having to lose a child, and at such a young age. I knew that these cases were possible, but actually working with these patients changed both my life and my outlook on nursing in the palliative care setting.

I started my engine and backed out of the driveway. Today was February 14, St. Valentine's Day. I thought how upsetting that every Valentine's Day would be a sad and depressing day for Louis's family in the future.

There had been a couple of inches of snow from an Alberta clipper this afternoon. The roads were somewhat covered but very manageable. I entered the highway and would be at my destination in forty minutes or so.

The radio was playing love songs the entire trip. Stevie Wonder's "Ribbon in the Sky" and Natalie Cole's "This Will Be." I hated it when the music never seemed to match what was running through my head with work.

As I turned onto Louis's street, I could see that the only house with lights on were his.

I parked my car and walked up to the front door. I knocked softly.

This was not my first visit to see Louis, so no introduction was needed.

"Hi, Pepper," James said, "right this way."

I quickly made my way to the den just off the living room. Louis was now staying in this room because he wanted to be close to the back of the house and near the backyard and pool. As I began the assessment, his mom, Janice, was present. She, as usual, had few words. She was stoic and almost seemed catatonic. She stayed for only a few more moments, and off she went to wherever it was she always escaped to.

Louis was nonresponsive, and his breathing was very shallow. His blood pressure was very low, and his heartbeat was faint. I repositioned him and delivered a small dose of liquid morphine for comfort. I also started him on oxygen to help his breathing.

I turned to James and explained to him that his son was very close to passing away.

James said, "Thank you for telling me. I'll let Janice know."

James left the room, and his son, to tell Louis's mother the devastating news. Janice returned and sat next to her son. She held his hand and kissed his forehead.

No words were spoken.

After a short period of time, Janice left the room once again and went to her "private place."

Time of death: 11:50 p.m.

Janice and James were given their privacy to say goodbye to their son.

Warm water was obtained, and the ritual began.

Once Louis was ready, James called the funeral home and thanked me repeatedly. Janice was nowhere close to her son, or me. I wanted to offer more comfort and ask if she needed anything else before I left.

I did not get the chance to see her again.

As a single man with no children of my own, I cannot imagine the loss of a child. I have read that the grief is probably the worst thing to endure. I felt like something was missing from this pronouncement.

It wasn't' complete.

I needed more closure. That even seemed selfish of me.

Six months had gone by since the death of Louis. I was now moving into my new house.

My best friend, Ann, called and said she wanted to stop by. She had something for me. I told her to come by that afternoon. When

Ann arrived, I saw she had two neatly wrapped presents. I could tell they were probably picture frames. The prints inside the frames were of beautiful tulips. One was dark green and white; the other was pink with a brown background.

"These will be perfect for my kitchen wall, opposite the large bay window," I said.

Ann agreed.

The two frames were hung without hesitation. Of course, being curious, I looked at the bottom of the two prints to see who created these lovely pieces of art.

I gasped. I was stunned.

Speechless.

There it was. The artist who painted the tulips for my new home was Janice Pall, Louis's mom.

I could not believe my eyes.

Without any knowledge of my caring for the child of this artist, and without even connecting the artist and the patient, my friend was able to bring emotional closure to myself and the mother of that young man. Mrs. Pall sent me a letter a few months later stating just that.

I looked up the telephone number for Janice and called to thank her.

When I called, James answered the phone. He informed me that Janice was still not speaking very much but that he would forward my thanks to her. He thanked me again, and we said our goodbyes for the last time. Apparently, drawing was an escape for Janice. Each time a nurse or home health aide came to visit Louis, she would paint. A world of artwork was her way to cope with what was unimaginable for a mother, and in her immense pain, she was able to make something beautiful.

The tulips still hang on my kitchen wall to this day!

EIGHT

A Grandmother's Love

Dispatcher call: "Patient has passed. Grandmother requesting pronouncement visit."

Two months prior to this request, I was sent to this home to perform extensive wound care and to treat anxiety and pain.

Julia, a thirty-eight-year-old woman, was admitted to hospice a few weeks before this visit. Diagnosis: HIV/AIDS. Julia had a long history of IV drug abuse. Her drug of choice was heroin. Because of her chronic drug use, Julia did not notice the usual symptoms of her infection. She was also negligent with any monitoring and treatment, leading to full-blown AIDS.

She was not married, the mother of two beautiful daughters named Amber and Alisha, and had a close bond with her grandmother Bessy. In recent years, Julia and her two girls moved in with Bessy. Before long, her grandmother discovered that Julia was using drugs again. Bessy offered her a choice: "Clean up or I will make you leave." Julia could not stop using drugs. Bessy finally asked her to move out and leave her two girls with their grandmother.

Julia left, not to be seen or heard from until three months ago.

The two-story condominium owned by Bessy was only a short distance from my home. During that first visit, I met Bessy, a very proud, self-sufficient woman with a difficult history of her own. She was eager to explain her granddaughter's past as well as her own.

They were very similar.

Bessy was a troubled young lady who became an adult in the 1960s. At that time, there was a lot of experimentation with drugs. Bessy became addicted to cocaine and LSD. She said she was very fortunate to have a strict father who took control of the situation and got her the help she needed to recover. Bessy went on to marry a man ten years her senior and had three children. One of her children, Roger, fathered a daughter, Julia. Roger disappeared from his daughter's life before her first birthday. Julia's mother died from a heroin overdose before she was five. Drug abuse ran rampant throughout this family, so Julia found it very difficult to avoid the downward spiral of drug use.

Julia was sent to live with a relative of her mother's, who was very irresponsible and neglected Julia's needs. Julia turned to drugs for escape.

Julia had different periods of her life when she was drug-free, and others when she was using. Somewhere in between, she gave birth to two daughters.

I rang the doorbell of the home, and Bessy answered.

"Hello," I said. "I'm Pepper, the hospice nurse."

"Hello. Please come in," Bessy replied. "I can take you upstairs to meet Julia, but may we talk first?"

"Of course," I answered.

Bessy and I connected immediately. She was warm and welcoming. A proud woman, who I sensed was very responsible and in charge of raising her two granddaughters. Amber was returning from an outing with her friends.

"Amber, say hello to Pepper. He is here to care for your mother," Bessy demanded.

"Hello, sir," Amber said.

"Hello, it is nice to meet you."

Bessy was going to make sure her granddaughters were well-mannered and well-behaved.

She believed it was her duty.

I walked upstairs to the room where Julia would spend her last days.

Julia was lying in bed, emaciated, now weighing just eighty-six pounds. Her expression was a combination of sadness, anxiety, and fear. Bessy introduced us.

"Julia, this is Pepper. He is the nurse who will care for you."

"Pepper, this is Julia, my sweet angel."

Julia was very weak and remained quiet during her assessment. Her breathing was very shallow, and she was complaining of severe pain in her lower back area. As I turned Julia to her side, she moaned in pain. What I saw were the worst skin issues I had ever seen in all the years of my practice.

Julia had multiple wounds on her buttocks. Each one was worse than the next. Each needed to be cleansed and have antibiotic creams applied every day. This caused a great deal of pain to Julia. It was sad to see that this young woman had AIDS, among several other problems she endured during her life. As I began treating her wounds, memories of my own youth emerged.

In the 1980s, I, like most people my age, was exploring our own sexuality and preferences. I was nineteen years old and working as a roulette dealer in Atlantic City at the Golden Nugget Casino. At that time, the AIDS epidemic was the disease we all feared most. I lost so many friends, and none of us knew at that time why or how all of that was happening.

Now here I was, even after all of these years, caring for a sweet child who was dying of the same horrible disease.

"Are you having any pain?"

"Yes, it hurts every time I move," Julia replied.

"I'm sorry. Let me administer a little morphine, and then I can continue once you feel more comfortable."

I administered the pain medication, and Julia and I talked some more. Julia started the conversation by expressing her regret for not being a better mother to her daughters. She felt weak, like a failure. I offered my support and attempted to ease her guilty feelings.

"We all make mistakes in our lives. It's important that you have some quality time with them. I think they will appreciate that."

"I hope so," Julia said.

Then as I was finishing the wound treatment, Julia slipped her tiny hand beneath the bed rail, gazed into my eyes, and whispered, "I am so scared."

I was speechless for a moment and on the verge of tears. It was the way she looked at me that brought me so close to breaking the professional standard that most nurses are taught to never cry in front of their patients or their families.

How could I tell her that death is not scary? I am not the person facing their own mortality. The best answer for something that I cannot explain is an apology.

"I am so sorry," I softly muttered. "Would you like me to stay with you for a while longer?"

"Yes." Julia seemed relieved and managed a little smile.

It actually is an honor to offer support to dying patients. It is what makes the job so satisfying. In a short while, Julia fell asleep and I left for home, but I was only to return a few weeks later.

As I drove to Bessy's condo, I felt all those same emotions that I felt during that first meeting.

I once had my own fears of the past involving possibly contracting AIDS. I recognized the absolute fear in Julia's eyes as she knew the pain she was going to experience through her death. As I started to travel, I needed to listen to music that was relevant. I popped in a CD that was my favorite during the time of my youth, Donna Summer's "MacArthur Park." As usual, it transported me back to that time, back to the clubs where I would spend endless hours partying and dancing. It was such a fun time, but the time before we knew how AIDS would kill thousands upon thousands of people. I parked my car in a visitor's spot and walked the sidewalk to the front door.

I didn't need to knock or ring the doorbell. The door opened, and Bessy greeted me.

"I just knew it would be you. I asked God to send you."

I went up to Julia's room to make the pronouncement. As I entered the room, I felt the silence, the emptiness, and the peace. I wondered if in that last minute she had felt fearful or scared. There was no one in the room except for Julia. No daughters, no neighbors, no one at all.

I could not help but think, *This poor child, who spent most of her adult life alone, is now alone in death.*

Time of death: 4:50 p.m.

Before I could ask, Bessy appeared in the doorway with a basin of warm water.

I was not surprised. Bessy struck me as a person who was well aware of what needed to be done, in life and after. I felt so relieved.

"Julia was so much more relaxed and accepting after your visit. She spent large amounts of time with Amber and Alisha."

"You truly are an angel," Bessy said with a big, satisfying smile.

"My work is almost complete now," Bessy said. "I am having Julia buried in the same cemetery and plot as my dead husband."

It was time to go downstairs and give the news to anyone who was waiting. Amber, Alisha, two neighbors, an Aunt, and a middle-aged African American man, who was introduced to me as Amber's biological father, had now arrived after I went to see Julia.

"I am sorry to have to tell you Julia has passed away."

Immediately, the room became chaotic.

Amber and Alisha were yelling and screaming, becoming inconsolable. Amber and Alisha's aunt collapsed on top of the two girls, moaning as she went down. The neighbors were silent, and Amber's biological father asked permission to see Julia. Bessy granted him that request.

I started by helping the aunt to get up to her feet. Then I consoled Julia's two daughters. They seemed to recover from the news more readily than the others. Bessy told me that this is how "we" get through the shock of death.

"I understand," I said.

Bessy asked me to stay with her until everyone calmed down a bit.

"Of course I will."

We sat and talked for over an hour. Bessy reminisced about happy times with her favorite granddaughter. Amber and Alisha listened attentively but really had little memory of their mother, only that they needed to love her for being their birth mother. As I stood to leave, Bessy gave me a tight hug and thanked me.

When I think of Julia, I think of the mothers across the world that struggle with addiction. My sister has been a neonatal nurse practitioner in Camden for over a decade, and she sees mothers that are addicts frequently. Certain parts of society may hate women like Julia, but I see that as ignorance. Addiction is a disease that kills and destroys like any other illness. I see Julia as a person who did make mistakes, instead of an addict, and I see her family as dysfunctional. But what family isn't? She did the best she could with all the factors playing against her, and I think that's admirable for her daughters, Amber and Alisha.

Her grandmother was there when she needed her the most.

NINE

Please Hurry!

Dispatcher: "Patient has passed away. Call daughter on the way."

I gathered my nurse bag and ran through raindrops to my car. It was a humid evening in July. During this trip, I chose to listen to a broadcast of the Philadelphia Phillies. It was the bottom of the fifth inning, and the Phillies were up 4–0. They were now in a rain delay.

The patient I was going to see was Rachel Labovitz, an eighty-seven-year-old Jewish woman who was suffering from congestive heart failure, a condition when the heart does not pump blood as well as it should. In her case, her condition was causing excess fluid to build up around her heart and lungs, making her very short of breath. Morphine was being administered; however, Rachel was not responding well to the medication. Her daughter had been calling three times a day every day this week for various problems and symptom management issues. Rachel was going to die.

As I was driving to the daughter's house, the rain intensified, and it became very hard to see the road. I needed to pull over and wait for the rain to subside. While parked on the shoulder of the road, I telephoned Rachel's daughter, Ellen.

"Hello," Ellen answered.

"Hello, my name is Pepper, the hospice nurse. I am on my way, but the rain is really coming down hard, and it is taking me longer than I thought. I will be there soon."

"Oh no! Please hurry. You must come quicker."

"I'm sorry. I thought Rachel had already passed?"

"Yes, she is gone. Just hurry."

The phone went silent.

As soon as the rain let up, I increased my speed and continued to the house.

The house was in the middle of an affluent neighborhood just before the Benjamin Franklin Bridge, which links South Jersey to Philadelphia, spanning over the Delaware River. House number 1700 has a wraparound driveway, water fountains flanking the north and south sides of the house, and very high double doors at the entrance. I noticed a funeral hearse just outside the front doors with a tall driver dressed in black waiting with the engine running. Before I could knock, the door flung open.

"Are you the hospice nurse?"

"Yes, I am…"

"Please come in and hurry up."

I was beginning to get suspicious about this "hurry up" request. The patient had already passed away. I was escorted through the ornate foyer with a large crystal chandelier hanging overhead. Once through that fancy entrance, I walked up several steps lined with mahogany wood spindles. Finally, down a long hallway to Rachel's bedroom. Once inside, I noticed the bed was stripped and my patient was nowhere to be found.

I was stunned.

Panic set in for a moment.

"Where is my patient?" I nervously asked.

"She is on the floor and ready to go," Ellen said.

"Did someone else come and pronounce her?"

"No, she is in the bag and ready to go with her driver."

"I need to make sure she is actually passed away."

"Fine, please make it quick."

"I am confused. What is going on here?"

Ellen, noticing my increased anxiety, and now suspicion, decided to explain to me what the "rush" was all about.

"My mother is Jewish," she began. "She was raised in Jerusalem along with her three sisters. It is Jewish tradition to bury the dead in as short a time as possible, typically before sundown the next day. My father is already buried in Jerusalem, and Mom requested we do the same for her. So as you can see, time is of the essence. That is why Mom is already in the cadaver bag and the limo driver is ready to transport her to the airport. Her flight leaves in less than an hour."

I answered by saying, "Thank you for explaining. Let me start the death certificate online. Could someone please bring me a basin of warm water?"

"Absolutely not!" she replied.

"My parents both wanted an ancient ritual performed for them once they passed away. It is called taharah, performed by a *chevra kadisha*. This is an organization of Jewish men and women who see to it that the bodies of deceased Jews are prepared for burial according to Jewish tradition and that they are protected from desecration. They are entrusted with the responsibility of showing proper respect for the bodies and the ritual of cleansing the body and subsequent dressing for burial."

The driver who was waiting outside was also going to be acting as a shomer, or watcher, to guard the body from theft or desecration until burial. He would drive Rachel to Philadelphia Airport and then escort her body to Jerusalem. Ellen added that these societies were formed into something called landsmanshaft fraternal societies in the late nineteenth century and early twentieth century.

Not all synagogues offer such services today.

"Oh, my apologies," I said.

"Not a problem," Ellen answered.

I finished the death certificate, and Rachel was soon on her way to the airport.

Time of death: 8:47 p.m.

Although my routine of washing the patient with warm water is an important part of my practice, I had to honor a religious tradition. It also helped to enlighten me more about other cultures in the world.

Baruch dayan emet.

TEN

Vietnam Soldier

Dispatcher call: "Our soldier has passed. Nurse visit requested by the daughter."

I had been to an apartment in Holman City to admit Tuan, a South Vietnamese army veteran who fought alongside American veterans against the North Vietnamese during that long and controversial war. Tuan, whose name translated means "bright" or "smart," was diagnosed with esophageal cancer two months ago. On admission, he had lost more than twenty pounds and now weighed a mere eighty-six pounds. He was only fifty-nine inches tall.

After the usual data gathering, assessment, and documentation, Tuan and I talked about his time in the war and how it affected his life. He explained to me that his country was completely torn apart by the battles being fought over those turbulent years. He went on to say that fighting with the American soldiers was an experience that changed his life forever. It was the main reason he eventually moved to New Jersey, started a vegetable produce business, and married his love, Lola. Lola was a cocktail waitress that Tuan had met in Japan while he was on leave following one of his tours.

Tuan explained to me that hospice was his best option for care during his final days because the Vietnamese believe they should die at home, surrounded by family and loved ones. It was very important to him that he not be a burden to anyone in his family.

Dispatcher call: "Tuan has passed away. Please pronounce."

As I started the engine of my car, I searched my CD collection for the soundtrack of *Miss Saigon*. This award-winning musical about the Vietnam War seemed appropriate for the ride to pronounce our soldier. The highway was bumper-to-bumper with early-morning drivers heading to work. The ride was long and tiresome. I sang along to "Why God Why?" and remembered seeing the show in New York City many years ago.

The apartment was located on the seventh floor, at the end of the hallway. One of Tuan's nephews greeted me in the lobby of the complex and escorted me in the elevator and to the apartment. Once inside, I noticed the changes made to the inside since my last visit.

Almost all the furniture was removed, except for the hospital bed our soldier was in. There was a large framed picture of Tuan in uniform from the time he served.

The smell of incense permeated the room.

As I approached the bed, I noticed a decent-sized bag sitting next to Tuan. Inside were articles of clothing, some personal items, and a small amount of cash. I also saw that someone had placed a handkerchief over Tuan's face, and there were gold coins in his mouth. I assumed this must be their tradition.

Just then, I heard his daughter, Linda, enter the room.

"Hi, Linda, I am so sorry for your loss," I said.

"Thank you for coming so early in the morning," she responded.

"Can you take this bag of things away so I can prepare your father for the funeral home?"

Linda, with tears in her eyes, said, "Those are the things that will go with Tuan."

"To the funeral home?"

"No, those items will go with him to the gods."

"And the coins?" I asked.

Linda now understood that I was very interested in the traditions and cultures of the patient.

She offered explanations.

"It is our belief that when a Vietnamese person passes away, his life has not ended. His afterlife begins. It is for this reason that certain essentials are prepared to go with our loved ones. Things like those in the bag. Next, we burn incense and say prayers. Today, we will have a religious leader come to offer prayers for my father."

I assessed Tuan for signs of life, but there were none.

Time of death: 8:45 a.m.

I requested the usual warm water and began preparing Tuan for the leader to view and offer his prayers.

Linda thanked me and offered additional information.

"Each year, on the anniversary of his death, we will have something called *dam gio*. This is a very festive celebration like a birthday party except it commemorates his date of death instead."

I thanked Linda for the very interesting lesson on Vietnamese culture and asked if there was anything else I could do for her.

She replied, "No, thank you so much again for all your help."

As I drove back home, I finished the soundtrack of *Miss Saigon*.

Tam biệt Tuan, and Cảm ơn.

ELEVEN

Edelweiss

Dispatcher call: "Wife of patient thinks her husband died."

I put my heavy winter coat on, with my favorite scarf and gloves, then headed out to my snow-covered car. It took more than thirty minutes to clean the ice and snow for me to begin my travel to Haddonfield for the pronouncement. The roads had yet to be cleared, and the snow was still coming down like a blizzard.

I turned down Becket Drive and started to slide, almost slipping by the house. The large two-story brick home sat a few hundred feet back from the street. There was a wraparound driveway lined with beautifully sculpted evergreen bushes, all leaning to the sides from the weight of all the heavy snow. I drove my car as close as I could to the entrance of the sidewalk that led directly to the front porch and, eventually, the large wooden door.

I rang the doorbell.

The door opened, and I was met by an elderly woman dressed in her nightgown. Her hair was tied in a striped bandana and pushed to her right side. She also looked as if she had not slept much lately.

"Hello, my name is Pepper. I'm the hospice nurse."

"Thank God. I'm Catherine. My husband Fritz is upstairs in the master bedroom. I don't think he is breathing," she replied.

WARM WATER

As Catherine walked me through the foyer and then the stairs, I noticed a beautiful glass display cabinet filled with multiple Hummel figurines. These porcelain treasures are based on sketches from Sister Maria Innocentia, a nun who lived in Germany in the 1930s. She drew the sketches for children. A local company began manufacturing them, and soon they became very popular among soldiers stationed in Germany after WWII.

Fritz was an air force pilot and was stationed in Frankfurt, Germany, after the war. He was engaged to Catherine and would send her a figurine once a month.

Catherine commented that those figurines represented the period of time she waited for her love to return. It also meant that each time one arrived, her Fritz was still alive.

I climbed the stairs and headed down the long hallway to the master bedroom. Once there, I could see Fritz was suffering and in a great deal of discomfort. He was not dead!

Fritz was diagnosed with bladder cancer one year ago. He did not undergo any aggressive treatment. Instead, he was admitted to hospice for comfort care. He suffered severe pain and discomfort on a daily basis. I immediately went to his bedside and inquired.

"Hi, Fritz, I'm Pepper. I'm here to take care of you. Where is your pain?"

"The pain is here." He pointed to his groin area. I could see that his diaper and bedsheets were soaked with bloody urine. I turned to Catherine and asked her how long he had been like this.

"I am not sure."

His blood pressure was very high, 188/90. An indicator of pain. I quickly located the morphine and administered a 20-milligram dose. I then began cleaning Fritz and asked his beloved wife for clean bed linens and clothes for after the bath.

Within a fairly short period of time, Fritz began to feel relief.

"I feel a little better. Thank you!" he stated. I administered a second dose of morphine, and Fritz fell asleep.

Catherine invited me downstairs and into the living room. Large leather sofas and love seats were perfectly placed along the pastel-colored painted walls. One wall immediately caught my eye. It was decorated with a series of paintings depicting scenes from the movie *The Sound of Music*. Catherine boasted about it and then showed me her original album personally signed by Julie Andrews. She continued, stating the movie was their favorite because it was so closely related to the era they met and of course Fritz's experience during the war.

Suddenly, we heard a cry from upstairs. Fritz was awake and obviously in pain. We both raced upstairs to rescue him from whatever symptom that he was experiencing. As I entered the room, I saw Fritz was halfway out of bed and delirious. He was holding his abdomen and crying in pain. Catherine and I helped him back into bed.

Additional doses of morphine and lorazepam were administered. Each repeated three times until Fritz fell into a deep sedation. I turned to Catherine and suggested she stay with her husband now.

I left the room to afford them some privacy. Before I left, I asked Catherine if there was anyone else she needed to call. Someone to be there with her to comfort her when the inevitable happens.

She answered me by saying, "We are alone. Our only son, Fritz Jr., died in an automobile accident many years ago."

"I'm so sorry," I replied.

I went downstairs and waited in the study while Catherine stayed with Fritz. I noticed a beautiful picture of the flower edelweiss. One like the one sung about in that famous movie. It was hanging next to a large portrait of a young man who I assume was their son, Fritz Jr.

Just then, Catherine called for me, saying, "Hurry."

As I entered the room, I could tell immediately that her love was gone. I listened for a heartbeat, breath, or any sign of life.

There were none.

Fritz was gone.

Time of death: 10:53 p.m.

Time for more warm water.

Catherine insisted on assisting me with the preparations. She explained to me that Fritz wanted to be buried with his only son.

I asked, "Where is Fritz Jr. buried?"

"In the homeland, of course."

"Germany."

I was confused. Homeland?

Catherine began to explain to me this mystery. Fritz was not an American soldier. He was a soldier from Germany. He was only seventeen years old when he voluntarily joined the German Army.

A decision he would regret the rest of his life.

It was something he would rarely talk about. He was ashamed. He sent those figurines home to Catherine every month as a gesture of beauty. He needed to convey some sense of goodness amid the terrible acts taking place overseas.

Catherine offered me one of those treasures. I declined. I explained that we are not allowed to accept any gifts from our patients or their families. I thanked her for the beautiful gesture.

I never thought that I would be taking care of a German soldier at any point of my career, but as nurses, we take the Florence Nightingale oath to help all of our patients regardless of their past histories.

TWELVE

Mom

The primary reason I became a hospice nurse was I had a personal experience with the death of my mother. Mom was diagnosed with stage IV lung cancer in the autumn of 2008. This was only a few months after she lost her younger sister Mary, who passed away from congestive heart failure. Mom had been a heavy cigarette smoker for more than fifty years.

Two of my siblings and I had also smoked cigarettes; however, we were able to successfully quit the health-damaging habit. Mom had tried, but she failed several times.

Now, it was too late.

Chemotherapy and radiation had temporary positive results. Mom was admitted to hospice in August 2009. At the time, it felt like we were giving up.

Throwing in the towel.

No more hope.

The reality was that treatment had failed, and this option would allow her to remain at home and have symptom management.

Joanne "Sissy" Cappuccio was a mother of five children: Michael (Pooch), Rose (Lynnie), Carol (Carrie), Barbara (Bobbie Dear), and

I, Carl (Pepper), the hospice nurse who had the honor of caring for each of the patients and families mentioned in this book.

Everyone has a nickname in our family.

Sissy was a schoolteacher for many years. She began her teaching years in Philadelphia and ended it in southern New Jersey. Her childhood was very difficult. Her father was an alcoholic and not a very good provider. Her mother worked at Connie Mack Stadium to ultimately support the five daughters. One of the few bright spots in Mom's childhood was her experience as a student while attending Little Flower High School in northern Philadelphia. During that time, she was influenced by one of her teachers, who introduced her to books, theater, opera, and the importance of world history. Her love of the arts and literature would be something she would share with her family, friends, and students for the rest of her life. This book is my way of paying respect and honor to one of the greatest influences in my life.

The last clinical intervention just prior to her admission to hospice was an ultrasound-guided fluid aspiration performed at the local hospital. Mom had several fluid drainings in the past few months. This time would be different.

I was present, along with my sister Lynnie and her son Stephen.

"Mom is here for her procedure," I stated to the unit secretary.

"Please have a seat and the doctor will be right with you," she replied cordially.

After a few moments, we were escorted to the procedure room with Mom. She was prepared for the needle injection as was done before. The ultrasound equipment was moved into place, and the doctor took a look at the images. He suddenly stopped and looked toward us with a very serious expression. We immediately sensed that bad news was coming.

"I am sorry to have to tell you this. There is very little fluid around your mom's lung. The space is almost entirely filled with cancerous tumors."

The first one to speak was Mom. "Well, I guess that's it," she responded.

Mom was well aware that this moment might come. She realized from the very beginning of her disease process that the outcome would not be positive. Being a devout Catholic, she accepted her fate as well as she could. My nephew, Stephen, began to cry, which in turn made his mother, Lynnie, cry, and of course myself as well. All of us were crying except for her. We arranged for ambulance transport for Mom's ride home.

That was the day we agreed on hospice.

The first nurse to visit mom was Vivian, a very calm, comforting nurse whom Mom immediately liked.

"I am Vivian. I will be your primary nurse while you are on hospice. I will be working with Debbie, also a nurse. She is friends with Pepper."

"Nice to meet you," Mom replied.

Vivian explained what tasks she would perform for Mom and how often she would visit.

Mom thanked Vivian and sent her on her way.

We are a very large family with many cousins and their spouses and numerous children of those cousins. Most of them consider our mom like a second mom. She represented stability to them, a source of calmness and comfort when necessary.

As soon as the word got out that Mom was on hospice, everyone wanted updates and time to visit.

Mom was very weak and not "in the mood" for many people visiting and fussing over her. She was the person of support, not the other way around.

The first week or so was fairly uneventful. Mom would stay on the couch, eat very little, sleep very little, and have visitors at her side most of the day. She had stopped doing the things she loved most during the past several months.

She stopped reading and writing in her diary and would not entertain the idea of taking a trip to her favorite place on earth: Disney World!

The one thing she did continue was *Jeopardy*. She watched almost every episode for more than twenty-five years. Now, in her weak state and lying on the couch, not looking at the television, she was still able to answer many questions correctly by listening to them.

Her mind was still intact.

This daily ritual was the last bit of normalcy that remained. It lasted for about three weeks, and suddenly, the end became much closer very quickly.

Throughout the few weeks that Mom was on hospice, Vivian and Debbie would spend extra time with me and others after caring for her. We would have easy conversations about Mom and what she was like, how she influenced us, her likes, dislikes, and so on. They were successful in getting me and other family members to open up about our inner thoughts and feelings about the loss we were about to experience.

They were starting the grief process.

Creating a path to healing before suffering that inevitable loss.

This is what attracted me to hospice nursing. The ability to connect with others during this sensitive time. An opportunity to grow and expand my own knowledge of the way other human beings react to impending death. Their own personal grief. And finally, their version of acceptance and a hope of survival. I incorporate a small discussion at the time of pronouncement to help the patient's loved ones begin the road to recovery.

I try to encourage the conversation to include memories of shared happiness. I usually simply ask a new widow or widower, "How long have you been together?" This simple question almost always gets someone to open up. It is so enlightening for me to listen. Oftentimes their stories are very similar and somehow connect back to me.

How fortunate for me to have a job that has such an impact on people who were total strangers just prior to this life-changing moment.

During the next several days, Mom became weaker, and her appetite diminished. She was sleeping most of the time, trying hard to respond to requests from loved ones who wanted to be near to her.

She was exhausted.

It all culminated on the anniversary of her mother's death. My mother's mom, Gertrude, died on August 26, 1987. It was late afternoon when Mom suddenly took a turn for the worse.

Mom could not breathe well and was having episodes of shortness of breath that required frequent large doses of morphine. It was my niece Jackie and I who administered those many doses throughout her last night.

It was the longest night of my life!

Mom was now lying in a hospital bed. Foley catheter in place. I could hear the humming of her oxygen concentrator as it was delivering fresh oxygen to her lungs. It was futile due to the blockage of her airway by a tumor. As I looked around, I noted the pictures of all Mom's grandchildren on the living room walls. I also spotted all the *Harry Potter* memorabilia sitting atop a CD storage case. A storage case filled with all of her favorite music. Opera choices of *La Boheme* and *Madame Butterfly*. Her favorite Broadway musicals, such as *The Phantom of the Opera, Les Miserables, Miss Saigon,* and *The King and I*. Next to the case was a long bookcase with sampling from her favorite authors. Mary Higgins Clark, John Grisham, and James Patterson.

Mom was never alone. She referred to her books and her music as her friends. Mom always said she never really needed to travel abroad.

"I have been around the world in my books," she would say.

As a small boy, my mother took me on those trips with her. She was a dreamer of sorts, a believer of all things good. Fantasy.

As I gazed around the room, I could barely see because there was always dim lighting in the room. The smell of nicotine still permeated the small apartment and was offensive as I sat there.

I did not mind. This was my mother. One who could do no wrong in my eyes.

I could tolerate the awful smell for a little while longer.

Mom was becoming more short of breath and the morphine increasingly more necessary for her comfort. The first few doses were very effective; however, as the night went on, the need to increase both dose amount and frequency was apparent.

"How do you feel?" I asked.

"A little better," Mom responded.

"You know, I love you very much." I felt I should say it now.

"I know. I love you too. I always knew my smoking would get me in the end," she admitted.

"It was your choice, no regrets," I encouraged her.

My mother was not the sentimental type. At least not openly. The few words spoken had to be concise. They were.

That was the most we said all through that last night. No long goodbyes were necessary. My mother and I were very close. Like soul mates, buddies, or friends. Anything that needed to be said had already been discussed.

My niece Jackie stayed with me throughout the night. She provided me with the emotional support I needed. She also assisted me with administering the morphine.

Twenty milligrams every hour.

At daybreak, Mom was still hanging on, barely. My three sisters arrived, each with their one daughter, to stay with Mom as I took some time to rest.

It was not very long until someone came and woke me from a twilight sleep to tell me that Mom had passed away.

I was told that Mom passed away just as she was being administered her "last rights." As the priest started the sacrament, Mom opened her eyes and lipped the words as he spoke. Just as the priest finished, Mom closed her eyes and her breathing stopped.

Mom was gone.

At peace.

No more suffering.

Time of death: 9:10 a.m.

The day Mom died was August 27, 2009. This would have been her eldest sister Barbara's seventy-sixth birthday.

Mom had already had her warm bath. It was completed by her very good friend Diana along with my youngest sister, Bobbie. Diana, who was much younger than Mom, had been like a fourth daughter to her. Diana spent several nights a week with my mother. Usually relaxing and watching television.

I will always be grateful for that assistance in that beautiful act of kindness from a person my mother loved.

Before I could clear my mind and understand what had just happened, there were several people climbing the stairs to say goodbye to Mom.

Multiple nieces and nephews. Her only surviving sister, Judy. An elderly aunt, Eleanor.

As fast as people were told the news, there were equal numbers of deliveries being sent to the apartment. A tray of homemade sandwiches, a fruit tray, multiple cakes, and trays of cookies. Pizza, meatballs, soft drinks, and on and on. It was almost an instant celebration.

So comforting.

Mom would have loved this for sure!

In a very short period of time, the funeral home was notified, and they were at the door. I needed to ask everyone to depart and move the "party" to another location.

After everyone was gone, I was alone with Mom and the funeral home staff.

They took special care to prepare Mom for the ride to the funeral home. I was doing just fine up until now. Not too anxious or tearful. It was not until I heard the front door close behind the two men carrying my mother out of her home that I completely fell apart. I cried out in inconsolable grief. Crying uncontrollably. Consoled by my mother's only surviving sister, Judy. She seemed to come out of nowhere to rescue me from a total breakdown.

I will always be grateful for that tender moment.

The next few days were filled with making arrangements for the funeral and remembering Mom. My niece Emily made a short video set to beautiful music, filled with many precious moments of Mom's life. This was shown at the funeral home as people were waiting to pay their respects to "Sissy."

The next day, we headed to the church for a Mass and then the cemetery for a Christian burial.

Family and friends filed into the church to celebrate Mom's life and reflect on the righteousness of her life. It gives us hope that our beloved Sissy would go to heaven. It is also very comforting to us as we reaffirm our own faith and belief.

Mom requested a selection from the movie *The Student Prince*. The song choice was "I'll Walk with God." I saw the movie several times with Mom. It was one of her favorites. It brought tears to many in the church that day.

Mom kept a daily diary for more than forty years. Each time a relative or loved one passed away, she would write, "May the souls of the faithful departed, through the mercy of God, rest in peace."

This is certainly the collective wish of anyone who loved my mom.

THIRTEEN

A Mother's Dilemma

Dispatcher call: "Patient is in severe pain, needs visit immediately."

I had just been watching a particularly funny episode of *The Golden Girls* before I received this call. It was the one where Blanche finds out that the IRS is auditing her. She eventually dresses up in one of her sexy nightgowns to greet the IRS agent at the door, only to be surprised that the agent is a woman. Watching this show puts me in a lighter spirit, and it also helps me to vent my sad emotions after going through a sad death.

It was a frigid night in February as I drove to a very rural area of South Jersey to see this patient who was in need. I decided to listen to talk radio that night, and there was a story on there about the upcoming election. It seemed that candidate Donald Trump was becoming more popular in the primaries in his quest for the Republican nomination; the radio station, which was a conservative outlet, was very pleased with the results thus far.

As I turned down the long dirt road to the home, I was careful not to skid into the frozen puddles that were forming in the road. The house was a hundred-year-old Victorian-style mansion with candlelights in all of the front widows. I walked up the stone steps, past the pillars, to the wide wooden doors. Before I could ring the doorbell, the door swung open to reveal a well-dressed middle-aged woman who had obviously been crying.

"Hi, I'm Pepper, the hospice nurse," I said.

"Hi, I'm Theresa, Angela's mother. Please come in. She's in the back room," Theresa said.

She led me through this huge house with several rooms before she led me to the back room, where Angela was lying in bed a few feet from the fireplace.

Angela was a twenty-eight-year-old patient who recently separated from her husband. She was diagnosed with an aggressive stage IV breast cancer four months ago. She had undergone chemo and radiation without any success, and now the doctors believed that she only had a few weeks to live. The cancer had spread to her bones and her lungs. She had excruciating pain in her back constantly. Angela was started on a morphine infusion two days ago; however, the pain was still persisting. My immediate job was to increase the rate of the infusion to attempt to control her pain. Her mother said that she was sleeping for the last twelve hours but waking up every fifteen minutes hollering in pain. As I adjusted the rate on the infusion pump, I told Angela what I was doing and offered additional emotional support. After around twenty minutes, she exhibited some relief.

She separated from her husband prior to the diagnosis, and she had a long history of alcohol abuse that led to some issues in the relationship. Her husband and her two children were now living in Upstate New York and were planning on visiting the next day. He had received full custody pending the finalization of the divorce, but everything was put on hold with Angela's health. It wasn't long before Angela started having significant relief from her pain and was able to talk.

"Hi, Angela, I'm Pepper, your nurse."

"Hi, I'm Angela," she said in a weak voice.

"Are you feeling any better?"

"A little."

"Can you rate your pain for me, 1–10?"

"It's about a 4."

Theresa came over with a glass of water for her daughter and used the remote for the bed to get Angela in a more comfortable position.

Then Angela turned to me.

"I have to ask a favor of you."

"How can I help?" I replied. Her eyes welled up with tears.

"How can I tell my two daughters that Mommy is going to die?"

I was stunned by this question, not sure how to respond.

"I can't imagine having to break that sort of news to your children. I can get a counselor to talk with you and be available when you do tell your kids. Would you like me to do that?"

She nodded her head as the tears continued to flow down her gaunt, pale face.

I, as a single man with no children of my own, could not begin to imagine the heartache this young woman was enduring. Her life was now about to end, and her one concern was the emotional burden her death would create for her two daughters. I made the request for the counselor who was available and went to my next nursing visit.

Two days later.

Dispatcher call: "Patient has died, nursing visit requested."

I immediately put on my heavy winter coat and started the drive to my patient. I selected the Carpenters CD from my collection. I needed to be calm upon arrival for this call. As I approached the property, I noticed several cars—BMW, Mercedes, and Lexus. The Lexus had a New York license plate. I walked up the stone steps and rang the doorbell.

After a few moments, the door opened, and I was greeted by a very pretty young girl of around twelve or thirteen years of age at most.

"Hi, I'm the hospice nurse."

"Hello, I'm Cindy. Please come in," she replied.

Cindy led me back to the room with the fireplace. There was a nice fire burning, and it was casting a shadow over the large throw rug that sat under the hospital bed. I could feel the warmth, smell the creosote escaping the chimney, and hear the cracking sound as the flames burned the dry wood.

It was then that I noticed the photos sitting on the hearth. They were of Angela and her two precious daughters. Photos of happy times over the years in no particular order. Photos from different periods of their lives—picnics, holidays, birthdays, and so on.

Cindy introduced me to her baby sister, Maggie.

"I am so sorry for your loss. Mom spoke very fondly of you both."

"Thank you."

I assessed Angela.

Time of death: 6:15 p.m.

I collected the washbasin and filled it with warm water. Bathed Angela and called the funeral home.

I offered a warm condolence to Theresa, a mother who had now lost her only child. Theresa, Cindy, and Maggie reminisced about their happy memories. They were extremely accepting and forgiving of their mother's weaknesses. They told me they suspected the end was near but were afraid to ask their mom. They respected whatever her wishes might be. They were very thankful for the support from the spiritual counselor. From across the room, I could see a young man weeping uncontrollably.

I walked over to offer emotional support.

Before I could begin, he stood to introduce himself.

"Hello, I'm Steve. I am Angela's soon-to-be-ex-husband, sorry, I guess, widower."

He began to cry again.

"I apologize for this. I am feeling just so sad right now."

I responded by explaining that grief can oftentimes make us angry, or sad, or upset, or, even a little guilty. Everyone deals with the loss of a loved one differently. It takes time to heal. I told Steve about our Grief Counseling Department to help loved ones through this very difficult time. I believed it would help him and his daughters to reach out. Steve agreed, and I forwarded a request to the Grief Center at work.

Cindy and Maggie interjected in the conversation, explaining that although their mom had her own demons to fight, she still managed to keep her daughters safe and well-adjusted. They were raised with good morals and self-esteem. They knew their mother loved them both.

They loved her as well.

No matter what.

FOURTEEN

Dignity and Respect

There was a torrential rainstorm happening outside as my evening shift began. I relaxed by sipping a fresh cappuccino. Suddenly, the message chimed on my work cell phone.

A patient in need.

Another family in crisis.

A fellow human nearing the end.

Dispatcher call: "Patient transfer from hospital. Death is imminent."

Leonard was a fifty-five-year-old retired food and beverage manager who worked in a few different Atlantic City casinos during the 1980s and 1990s. He fell victim to the fast-paced lifestyle of the time period. Leonard drank alcohol almost every night in the local bars and nightclubs. He was reckless and lived through two bad marriages. He did manage to produce a lovely daughter from one of his wives. Her name is Katherine.

Katherine lived just a few miles west of Atlantic City, in a second-floor apartment. Her dad had a condo just a few miles from her and now shared his life with Barbara, a retired roulette dealer from the Golden Nugget Casino.

I darted across my front sidewalk to my car, trying to avoid as many raindrops as possible before I entered my car, which turned out to be an exercise in futility. I quickly opened the car door and sat in the seat. I carefully wiped my computer of the water and secured myself with seat belts.

As I began the slow ride down the pike, I tuned my radio to a soft rock station. Celine Dion was singing one of her top songs. Ironically, it was the theme from *Titanic*. I sang along.

I arrived at Leonard's condo just as the ambulance was pulling into the parking lot. The rain was still pounding the asphalt and creating puddles the size of swimming pools. I watched as the paramedics carefully lifted Leonard from the ambulance on a stretcher. They covered his entire body with extra sheets in an attempt to keep him dry. Step-by-step, they walked him into the condo and transferred him to his hospital bed.

Leonard was very weak, ashen, and barely breathing. At first glance, one might think this person has passed away.

I introduced myself to the patient's girlfriend, Barbara, and the daughter, Katherine.

"Hi, I'm Pepper, the hospice nurse. I am going to admit Leonard and see that he has everything he needs for tonight."

They both were very grateful that I was there and had some questions for me.

"How long do you think he might survive?" asked his daughter.

"I do not know. I'm sorry. I don't usually try to predict. My stock answer is that 'only the man upstairs knows when that might happen.'"

"Thank you for being up-front."

As we were talking, the paramedics were moving their equipment out of the condo and leaving.

I asked, "Can you help me reposition the patient and then you can leave?"

They apologized and said they really had to be on their way. One of them did help me move Leonard up in the bed.

Once I removed the bed linens from the patient, I was stunned to see that Leonard was soiled. There was dried excrement on his buttocks that looked like it was not attended to in a long time.

I asked Katherine to fill the basin with warm water and to bring me some clean wash clothes and dry towels. I proceeded to wash Leonard and remove all soiled material from him.

Katherine noticed what I was doing and asked, "What is that all about?"

I said, "That is neglect. Not to worry. I will make him comfortable and have him cleaned up in no time."

Katherine expressed great appreciation when I was finished. Tears filled her eyes as she watched her father struggle to breathe.

I administered 20 milligrams of morphine under his tongue and repositioned him one more time.

As soon as I was finished, I instructed both Katherine and Barbara to call the 800 phone number with any concerns.

I drove back home. The rain had now stopped; I left the music off. I remember thinking it was the least I could do to extend some sort of dignity and respect to Leonard.

As the sun was rising, my phone chimed again.

Dispatcher: "Leonard has died. Please pronounce."

The drive seemed so much shorter this time. Again, no music playing. The road was deserted, and no residual water was seen from the recent deluge of rain the night before. I arrived in under thirty minutes.

I walked into the condo and Leonard was silent.

Gone.

Breathing had ceased.

Barbara was alone now. Katherine had gone home for rest and had to watch her two children before they went to school.

Barbara thanked me for all I had done the night before. She believed that I made the end a little more tolerable for Leonard.

I asked, "How long were you and Leonard together?"

Barbara began reminiscing.

"Leo and I met at a mutual friend's funeral. He was still drinking at that time. The death of his friend woke him up. He started going to Alcoholics Anonymous. He has been sober for around three years now. Last January, Leo was diagnosed with stage IV liver cancer. Nothing could be done. He only lasted six months."

"What am I going to do without my Leo?"

I hugged Barbara and offered my heartfelt condolences as always.

The patient was still clean and ready to go from his warm bath earlier.

Time of death: 6:15 a.m.

Later that same day, an e-mail from my manager was sent to me and virtually everyone else in my hospice organization.

The daughter of Leonard M., Katherine, sent this beautiful letter of gratitude about Pepper, her father's nurse.

> Pepper bathed my father last night as he came home soiled and uncomfortable. He was gentle and thorough in his care. Pepper then sat with us and explained the signs and symptoms of dying. He made a very sad situation "warm, caring, and even happy." It was what my father wanted, dignity and respect, and to be able to die at home. I will never forget what Pepper did for my father.

This is why I do what I do.

To have a lasting positive impact on the lives of others as they navigate through these tough times.

FIFTEEN

The Girls of Spring

Dispatcher call: "Patient in decline. Daughter requesting visit."

It was the start of a new shift, a new week, a new patient in need, and a family to console.

I gathered my nurse bag, a bottle of water, and a small bag of Weight Watchers chips. I started on the "new" program around one year ago. To date, I am down almost forty pounds. Feeling more energetic and light, I easily sprinted to my car in the driveway to begin the drive to my next unfortunate sick and dying patient.

I started the engine, popped in a hot new CD, Bruno Mars. I sang along to "Uptown Funk: as I sped along the Atlantic City Expressway toward a small city just east of the Ben Franklin Bridge.

I exited the road and onto Grape Street to the last house on the corner, number 3213. It was a two-story Victorian-style walk-up. There were several children playing in the front yard and several adult men standing around or sitting on the porch. All of them looked related, possibly brothers. Most with distinct oval-shaped blue eyes, long narrow noses, square jawlines, and pale skin tones. There looked to be at least nine or ten of them, huddled together, some clutching half-empty beer bottles.

I made my way to the steps and introduced myself.

"Good morning, I am Pepper, the hospice nurse."

"Mornin' to you, sir, we are June's brothers."

"All of you?" I managed to stammer out.

"Yes, friend. We are ten in all. Lost Patrick a few years ago to cancer, just like our June."

Each man was sure to introduce themselves to me as I shook the hand of each one of them. Brian, James, Jack, Sean, William, Connor, Daniel, Noah, Finn, and Brody. They ranged in age from fifty-four to seventy-six.

What a polite group of siblings, united in support of the family during this difficult time. As I passed through this group of gatekeepers, I walked through the ordinary front door. Inside, I was greeted by the patient's daughter; her name was also June.

"Hi, I'm Pepper, the nurse. I'm here to see Mom."

"Thank you so much for coming so quickly. Mom is in the bedroom in the rear of the house. Let me take you there."

The entire house was decorated shabby chic. It had emphasized vintage elements to recreate the antique flea market look. Most of the furniture was characterized by an aged appearance, with distressed wood composition in sanded milk paint to show signs of wear and tear. Most of the colors were white, ecru, and pastel with just a hint of vibrant colors here and there. The air was scented lilac from soft candles burning in the corners of the rooms. I remember hearing Anthony Kearns singing one of his signature songs as it echoed throughout the home. I followed young June into the bedroom and was introduced to her mom, June, who was in bed and obviously struggling to breathe.

June, the patient, was a seventy-seven-year-old woman dying of pulmonary hypertension. She was diagnosed almost five years ago and, since then, had become increasingly more dependent on oxygen and other powerful narcotics to relieve her constant shortness of breath. June lost her husband to heart failure almost ten years ago. So far, today, June had been administered multiple doses of morphine, with little success.

Although in respiratory distress, June managed a broad, inviting smile and asked me to join her at the bedside.

I accepted the invitation willingly.

"Hi, I am Pepper, your nurse."

"Hello, Pepper, I am sorry to say that this may be my end. What can you do for me? The plan so far is not working. Morphine is not doing the trick. I cannot catch my breath. Please make it better!"

"Well, June, I want to administer a larger dose of morphine. I am also going to administer lorazepam to help reduce your anxiety."

June was too weak and short of breath to continue talking. She nodded her head in agreement to receive her medications.

The first dose seemed to help, however, not enough to achieve comfort. It took several doses of each, morphine and lorazepam, to finally make June comfortable. Unfortunately, it also placed her in a sedated state. She would not speak again.

Not respond to her loved ones.

Be silent forever.

As June slipped into her dream state, her daughter, June, began to weep. The end was so near, and she felt a great loss.

Time to console.

I explained to June that her mother was much more comfortable in this state and would be able to make that final journey with ease.

"I can't imagine what you are feeling now, but this is the best thing we can do for her."

I asked June how amazing it must have been growing up with so many uncles. She laughed and said it was always difficult to get a word in when they were all together. I asked her if she had any aunts, afraid to hear the answer after all those uncles out on the porch.

June said, "Mom is one of fourteen children, eleven brothers and two sisters. Of course, one brother had passed away recently, Patrick."

I asked, "Where are her two sisters now?"

June said, "They both live in California and would be flying in tomorrow morning."

"There is a photo right here on this wall."

I walked over to the small photo on the wall just above June's dresser. There they were, all three sisters, smiling for a picture taken in front of Cinderella Castle in Disney World in Florida.

"May I ask their names?"

"Sure. That is mom, June, in the middle. On her right is April, and on her left is May."

April, May, and June.

Unbelievable.

Just as I was surprised by the sisters' names, I heard a few last gasps of breath from my patient.

June was gone.

Time of death: 5:55 p.m.

I requested the usual basin of warm water from June's daughter. She happily brought the basin to me and actually helped with the postmortem ritual.

I then went out and invited the ten brothers in to say goodbye to their sister.

One by one, each brother placed their hand on their beloved sister, and each kissed her forehead. Some were stoic and some openly cried.

I consoled each as best I could. It was very moving.

Brian, the eldest of the patient's sons, invited me to attend June's traditional "Irish wake." This was, and still, is a custom of most Celtic countries. It is rooted in the idea that mourners would keep vigil or watch over the dead body until burial. This is the "wake." Oftentimes the wake is a celebration of sorts where families and friends can gather, eat, drink, and share memories. It forced me to recall a memory I had of an Irish uncle who passed away more than forty years ago. He was a retired Tastykake employee who would visit once in a while and bring us our favorite treats. Mine were mini powdered donuts.

On the night of the viewing, I remember sitting in the velvet chairs in the main sitting room at the funeral parlor. One by one, relatives and friends filed past the coffin to pay respects to Uncle Jack. The parlor was soon filled with more than fifty people, all conversing. Some tearful, some exchanging pleasantries, all loud.

All of a sudden, the room was almost empty. I asked my mother, "Where is everyone?"

My mother chuckled and answered, "They are all across the street drinking and partying."

I accepted the invitation from Brian and was soon on my way home.

SIXTEEN

I'll Walk with God

Rosa was a ninety-year-old widow with severe congestive heart failure. I was conducting a home hospice evaluation so Rosa could be discharged to her home and die a peaceful and dignified death. At the bedside, sitting and listening very attentively, was Rosa's daughter, Alberta. Alberta was a sixty-two-year-old woman who never married. She literally had spent her entire adult life caring for her widowed mother. Rosa had had mild dementia and heart failure for almost thirty-five years.

"Hi," I introduced myself. "I'm Pepper. I am a nurse and will be talking with you about Rosa, your mom."

"Hello, I'm Alberta. I'm the sole caregiver for my mom." She was fighting back tears.

Alberta, being a devout Catholic, stated, "It's my responsibility. You can't abandon family."

I requested information about Rosa from the unit secretary. I then explained the philosophy of hospice. When I finished, Alberta, now very emotional, signed the consent papers and designated Rosa DNR (do not resuscitate). Alberta decided that "heroic measures are not warranted at this time."

WARM WATER

The admission was arranged for when Rosa was discharged. I said goodbye to Alberta and told her that a different nurse would arrive at the house after Rosa got home, and they would finish the admission.

"Thank you," said Alberta.

I replied, "You are very welcome."

I went home to document the nursing visit on my computer.

It was an unusually mild Saturday morning in January. I was up early and began walking my two shih tzus, Stella and Jake. They were always eager to walk around the neighborhood and flirt with the neighbors. Jake is the shy one; Stella is very forward and a handful for sure.

Dispatcher call: "Patient not doing well, daughter not coping, needs a visit now."

I put on my gray Banana Republic button-down jacket and headed out to my car. I had a slow night and actually slept for nearly six hours straight. I was well rested. It must have rained during the night because I noticed the front sidewalk was still darkened from moisture, and the grass was damp as evidenced by how wet my black Avani shoes were as I got in the driver's seat and started the engine. I turned on the radio and listened to Sid Mark as he introduced song after song from the one and only Frank Sinatra. I loved to tune in every weekend for this Philadelphia tradition. "The Lady Is a Tramp" and "Night and Day" played back-to-back. It doesn't get any better than this.

Traffic was always light on the weekend, so I arrived on Forest Lane rather quick. The development was only a few years old. It was a long, continuing row of town houses. The builders chose this style of urban construction because of the limited space. All were two stories with traditional layouts with minimal lawn space. The winding sidewalk leading to the front door was flanked with beautifully sculpted evergreen bushes. A huge Christmas wreath still hung on the front door.

I pushed the Blink doorbell, and immediately, Alberta ran toward me to let me in.

"Pepper," she stammered out. "I am so glad it is you. Mom is not doing well. Come upstairs with me, and maybe you can help her."

As I passed through the living room, I couldn't help notice how beautiful the town house was decorated. The living room was done in light gray-and-white floors, and there were small sofas along with splashes of red evenly placed around on glass tables. As I made my way toward the steps leading to Rosa's room, I went through the dining area just off the kitchen. This room had an open ceiling that extended from the lowest point in the home to the highest. Covering all the walls were replicas of works by famous artists.

Some of the replicas included Claude Monet, Vincent van Gogh, Leonardo da Vinci, and Raphael. The creations included *Mona Lisa*, *The Last Supper*, and *The Starry Night*. It turns out Alberta is an interior decorator with a keen eye.

I quickly followed Alberta upstairs and into her mother's bedroom. Once there, she began sobbing and explaining to me all that was happening with Mom.

"She started breathing hard this morning, and she won't wake up!" she began.

"What medications have you given her?" I asked.

I could see at a glance that Rosa was in respiratory distress. I could hear audible wheezing and secretions without the use of my stethoscope. Her face was flushed, and she was very restless as she lay in her bed.

Alberta said, "I gave her one dose of morphine."

Rosa was starting her last journey.

"I will give her a large dose of morphine along with lorazepam to calm her anxiety. I am also going to give her Levsin, a medication to help reduce the secretions in her throat," I said.

"Thank you. Then I will give Mom her daily bath and change the sheets."

On observation, the patient was clean and was lying on top of beautiful, clean sheets that looked like they were pressed. I did not object. I agreed to assist Alberta with her duties.

WARM WATER

I watched in amazement as she carefully undressed her mother, being sure not to leave private body parts exposed, especially to me. She went to the bathroom and returned with a basin of warm water, lilac-scented soap (her mother's favorite), and fresh warm towels for drying.

This tender display of compassion and respect continued.

Once clean and dry, Alberta began moistening her mother's skin with Jergens lotion and even filed a few of her nails.

Finally, the bed linens were changed, including fresh pillowcases.

All throughout this process, Alberta talked to her mother through her tears, as if Rosa were completely awake and aware of what was being done for her.

I explained to Alberta that Rosa was very near death. I was surprised that her mother had not passed away while I was there.

Alberta thanked me for helping her and stated she would call the service if anything "happened."

I drove home and was greeted by my two babies, Jake and Stella.

After just a short period of time,

Dispatcher call: "Alberta called, Rosa has stopped breathing. Need nurse now. Please send Pepper."

I quickly went to my car and began my return trip.

This time, Alberta did not meet me at the door. I was greeted by her sister, Diana. She was tearful as she introduced herself.

"Hi, I'm Diana, Alberta's sister. She is upstairs with Mom. Follow me."

Without hesitation, I followed Diana upstairs. Once there, I offered my condolences.

"I'm Pepper. I was here with Alberta earlier. I am so sorry for your loss."

"I know who you are. My sister told me all about you. Thank you for helping her with Mom. I know she really appreciated it."

"You are both welcome."

As I was talking with Diana, I noticed there was beautiful music being played throughout the entire house via intercom.

"Come Prima, Come Prima, I'm in love."

It was one of my mother's favorite singers, Mario Lanza.

It transported me back to my childhood when we would listen to music. My mother introduced me, my siblings, and many others to art and culture. The joys of music, reading, learning about different places around the world.

I was remembering and feeling emotional.

Just then, the song changed.

"I'll Walk with God." A song from the movie *The Student Prince*. Starring Mario. It was also a song my mother insisted be played at her funeral.

Now I began to cry. I cried at the memory of my beloved mother. Cried for Alberta, who demonstrated such love and respect for her mother. Cried for any child who has to say goodbye to a parent.

Time of death: 2:05 p.m.

It was so nice to know that I needn't ask for the basin. Alberta was already getting the warm water.

We went through the entire ritual as completed earlier. I did not mind. I got to hear several more songs by Mr. Lanza.

After calling the funeral home, Alberta and I talked for a while.

We talked about travel destinations we had in common. We both have traveled to England and France. She had seen the Vatican; I had not.

Although Alberta had given up most of her adult life caring for her mother, she had no regrets. She accepted her place in life and did what she had to do. She loved her mother very much.

I asked Alberta what she will do after everything calms down and she is free to do anything she wants. Her answer was simple. "I'll live," she said with a satisfying smile.

SEVENTEEN

So Young

I had a very easy night on call. No nursing visits since 7:00 p.m. the night before. This morning, the temperature was above normal, and the sun was shining bright.

Dispatcher call: "Husband of patient called, his wife has passed."

I arose quickly and washed my face, and out the door I went. Nursing bag, cell phones, and coffee in hand. The morning news was on the radio. I listened for a short while and then turned the dial to listen to soft rock. Elton John, Barry Manilow, and Barbara Streisand. Traffic was heavy as usual for the morning rush. It seemed to be moving extra slow today. School buses and delivery vans all competed with workers trying to get to work on time.

I never like to make a caregiver wait too long for my arrival. It is such a sad time for them.

I took the exit off of Route 42 onto Coles Road. In a few miles, I turned onto Green Street, house number 1700. The home was a charming cottage in a quiet suburban neighborhood overlooking a lake. It was close to the elementary school and within walking distance to the food market. The house was among several other similarly built homes that lined both sides of the street. It was obviously an affluent neighborhood as evidenced by the beautifully landscaped lawns and expensive cars in each driveway.

I parked on the street just outside the gate to the driveway. I walked to the front door and rang the doorbell.

I was greeted by a family friend.

"Hello, I am Pepper, the hospice nurse," I said.

"Hi, I'm Veronica. Please follow me."

I entered the foyer and noticed a ten-foot-tall ancient grandfather clock on the left side of the room on the way to the living room. The cathedral ceilings created an echo from the hardwood floors as I walked through the house to see my patient.

As I entered the bedroom, a handsome young man stood and introduced himself.

"Hi, I'm Edwin. Thank you for coming. This is Nancy, my wife. She passed away just after seven this morning." Tears were streaming down his face.

"I am so sorry for your loss," I managed to state, noting how young Edwin was.

I then turned to look at Nancy, Edwin's deceased wife.

I was stunned!

Nancy was only forty-two years old. A victim of advanced breast cancer. She had a very long and hard battle with her disease. Nancy was diagnosed more than five years ago with stage IV breast cancer. Chemotherapy and radiation added these many more years to her life, but it was difficult. Just four weeks ago, Nancy decided to be admitted to hospice and end her days at home with her family.

Her family included her husband, Edwin, and her seven-year-old daughter, Lisa Marie.

I listened to her heartbeat; there was none.

I checked her respirations; there were none.

Nancy has died.

Gone to heaven.

Passed away.

Made her daughter motherless.

Time of death: 9:25 a.m.

I asked Edwin, "Where is your daughter?"

"She is upstairs playing in her room. I am not sure how she will take this," he replied.

"May I request someone from the office who is more familiar with dealing with children at a time like this?" I implored.

"No," Edwin immediately said. "I don't want Lisa Marie to be exposed to this. She kissed her mommy goodbye last night, and I want her to remember that moment."

I complied with Edwin's request and asked the family friend for a basin of warm water as per usual. Her friend insisted on helping me with the ritual. I welcomed her help. We washed Nancy and dressed her in a light-blue dress provided by Edwin.

The funeral home was notified, and they were on their way.

I again offered condolences to Edwin and provided emotional support as I attempted to start a conversation.

"How long have you and Nancy known each other?"

That was all I needed to ask. Edwin was so eager to tell me his and Nancy's story. His way of talking it out.

This would begin his journey of recovery.

"Nancy and I first met at a high school dance, almost twenty-five years ago," he stated. "I know it sounds old-fashioned or naive. That was where it all began. Nancy was sixteen, and I seventeen. We both seemed to sense immediately that we were soul mates. You know, laugh at the same things, answer each other's questions before they are asked. Kismet! We waited until Nancy finished law school to get married. It was a beautiful day in June. Nancy was such a beautiful bride. It feels like it was so long ago."

Edwin's face was soaked with tears, as was mine.

I could not imagine the sadness he felt.

Just then, there was a knock on the door. It was the funeral home to take Nancy.

Edwin bent over to give one last loving kiss before the woman he loved, the mother of his child, his everything, was taken away.

The funeral home staff was very careful to place Nancy in a cadaver bag before placing her on the stretcher for transport. I requested they not close the bag until they were out of the house.

They complied. Once Nancy was gone, I again provided emotional support to Edwin.

"Thank you for everything," he said.

"It was my honor to help you. I am so sorry. If you need anything, please do not hesitate to call."

I usually am able to handle most situations with a reassuring calmness. This case was very emotionally draining. When I have to pronounce a very young patient, I can't help but feel they were cheated. Taken too soon, so it seemed unfair.

As I started to drive off, I tuned the radio to a pop station. Bruno Mars, Shawn Mendes, and Ariana Grande belted out recent releases. I could feel myself relaxing and anticipated going home to be with my two pets, Jake and Stella.

It wasn't too long before my rejuvenating experience was interrupted.

Dispatcher call: "Caregiver requesting nursing visit, patient passed away."

I confirmed receipt of the call and set my GPS to the new address. This patient lived just six miles from the last. I noticed the rush-hour traffic was now over, and the ride was fairly quick. I turned off the highway once again, and within a few minutes, I arrived at the new address.

Number 8143 Olive Lane, trailer number 23. Trailer after trailer sat a few feet back from the poorly maintained asphalt roadway. The small lawns consisted of crabgrass and weeds. Most of the trailers had filthy exteriors, and hardly anyone had a vehicle. The few children I saw outside were dressed in shabby, unclean clothes and unsupervised.

A much different neighborhood from the previous one!

I spotted number 23 and got out of my car to knock on the door. I was greeted by a young woman dressed in a short skirt layered with an oversized sweater.

"Hi, I'm the hospice nurse, Pepper."

"Hello, I'm Suzie, James's sister," was her reply. "Please come in."

As I entered the trailer, I was met with an all-too-familiar smell of old cigarettes. Being an ex-smoker, I recognized this scent imme-

WARM WATER

diately. As my eyes scanned the trailer, I noted a very untidy living space. Dirty dishes piled in the sink, old worn furniture with multiple stains from spilled drinks and food. I could barely see because of poor lighting and dark window treatments. There was a scrawny gray-haired cat perched on the back of one of those sofas. It jumped and screeched as I made my way toward the back of the trailer to the bedroom.

Suzie said, "Here is my brother. I think he stopped breathing."

"Thank you, Suzie," I managed to blurt out.

As I looked at James in the bed, I was once again stunned at the young appearance of the newly deceased.

Two in the same morning.

Two young adults passed away way too soon.

James was thirty-five years old. He had been a very heavy smoker most of his young life. He was very poor and never had good health insurance. He waited until his symptoms were too much to handle before getting tested. By then, the lung cancer had spread to his liver and brain. Suzie was his primary caregiver and needed a lot of support caring for her brother. There were no other family members available to assist her during this time.

I checked James for a heartbeat and respirations; there were none.

He was gone.

Time of death: 11:10 a.m.

James was in his own bed, sheets half off the bed, and no pillowcases on the pillows. He was lying there in his underwear, no blanket.

He was filthy!

I asked Suzie to bring me a basin of warm water and soap. I also inquired if she had a clean washcloth and towel. Once she brought those, I asked her to locate clean sheets and pillowcases. I even suggested looking for some clean clothes for James.

I gave James a complete bath, dressed him in his favorite gym shorts and top, placed the best sheets Suzie could find and pillowcases.

James was now ready for the funeral home.

I turned to Suzie to ask if I could help with calling the funeral home. She was now sobbing uncontrollably.

"He never looked so good. Thank you so much."

"My pleasure," I answered.

Suzie continued, "James was always a loner. He kept to himself. Never had much luck with the ladies. He just was happy to work his forty hours a week and relax on the weekend. That meant sitting at the local bar Fridays and Saturdays until closing. Drinking and smoking all night. The bar was just down the street outside the trailer park. James never drove while he was drunk."

Simple life, no complications.

Happy the way things were.

Now he was dead at a young age. I didn't understand.

For the second time this morning, I was basically speechless. What could I offer as an explanation to this sweet child?

I decided that the best way to approach Suzie was to reinforce the praise she deserved for being a wonderful caregiver to James.

"Suzie," I began, "James was so lucky to have you taking care of him."

I remembered that along with the clutter I noticed on the way through the trailer, I also noticed a large crucifix hanging over James's bed. There was also a statue of the Blessed Mother on top of the old dresser next to his bed.

I asked Suzie, "Was James a religious man?"

"Oh yes, he was," she replied, "a devout Catholic."

"I am also Catholic. I know sometimes it can be difficult to understand God's plan, but there is always a plan."

I don't usually offer rational reasons for why a young person passes away so early. I felt I needed to give Suzie something to hold on to.

Suzie wiped her tears away and looked me right in my eye and said, "Pepper, you are an angel. Thank you so much."

That was all that needed to be said. I hugged Suzie and was on my way home.

Driving home, I left the radio off and just let my mind wander. This morning I pronounced two young people. One wealthy, one poor, one male, one female. One with a lot of resources and support, and the other almost alone and destitute. One never mentioned faith, and the other a devout Catholic.

It is my job to treat each patient and their loved ones with equal respect and dignity. I strive to do this each and every day.

When someone calls me an angel, I am embarrassed. The newly deceased are the angels. I believe they have just gotten their wings.

The job I perform is rewarding and satisfying. I help these families begin a journey to recovery after they lose a loved one.

I'm grateful for that every day!

EIGHTEEN

Valentine's Day

Friday was a very cold February day. The air was crisp, and there was no air movement at all. The winter had been unusually warm until today, and I had no complaints. I moved back to New Jersey from South Florida a few years ago. I just could not take these long, harsh winters like I used to. I'm still single, so I offered to cover the night shift so the lovers on the staff could enjoy a night out on the town.

The calls began early.

Dispatcher call: "Patient passed, wife requesting a nurse."

The air was so cold I needed extra layers of clothing. The first was my uniform. This was a light-blue pullover top and black dress pants. I added a wool sweater. Finally, my Eddie Bauer down jacket with scarf and gloves.

I ran quickly from my front door to my car, which was already warming up. I started it with my remote control. The radio was on, and my usual soft rock station was playing one love song after another. Blake Shelton's "God Gave Me You" and John Legend's, "You and I" played back-to-back.

The roads were filled with people traveling to and from their night out. It took extra time to drive to my first assignment. It was a small row home in Gloucester City, a small city that is literally located under the Walt Whitman Bridge. It is a very poor city with a higher-than-average crime rate. I managed to find a parking spot at the end of the block. I closed my jacket as much as I could and braced myself for the cold walk to the house.

I knocked on the door and waited for an answer.

The door opened, and I was greeted by Eleanor, a ninety-five-year-old woman who stood only five feet at most and could not weigh more than one hundred pounds.

"Hi, I'm Pepper, the nurse," I managed to state.

"Oh, please come right in. I'm Eleanor. Joe is right in here."

Eleanor led me to the back of the row home to where her husband, Joe, was being cared for.

"Here he is. I tried waking him this morning, and he didn't answer me. He always answers me right away."

I could tell immediately that Joe had probably been dead for several hours. Eleanor must have woken him up this morning and didn't realize that he had passed away during the night.

Joe, an army veteran, was diagnosed with end-stage renal disease three years ago. He had been on dialysis three times a week for the past two. Joe was ninety-eight years old and could barely tolerate the treatment. It probably shortened his life rather than prolong.

I performed the usual tests—heartbeat, respirations, and so forth.

Joe was gone.

Hopefully to heaven, as Eleanor wished.

Once I officially pronounced and Eleanor processed the situation, she took out her rosary and began praying. She asked me, "Are you Catholic?"

I said, "Yes, I am."

Eleanor requested that I say at least one prayer with her.

I agreed.

We both started together:

"Hail Mary, full of Grace. The Lord is with thee. Blessed art thou among women, and blessed is the fruit of thy womb, Jesus. Holy Mary, Mother of God, pray for us sinners, now and at the hour of our death. Amen."

I could sense a strength in Eleanor. A strength enforced by her faith.

Time of death was 6:45 p.m.

I asked Eleanor if I could start the postmortem care.

She replied, "Yes, let me fill the sink with warm water."

In all the time I had been doing pronouncements, that was the first time someone initiated the ritual that I hold so dear to me. That last act of compassion.

This was so beautiful.

Eleanor also insisted that she help me wash Joe. As we started, she began to tell me their story.

"Joe and I met at the Marlborough-Blenheim Hotel in Atlantic City in 1940. I was out with my girlfriends on a Friday night. Back then, it was rare to be out with just the girls. It was a grandeur time of Atlantic City, and ladies were to be escorted by gentlemen. That was the opening line from Joe."

"A beautiful lady such as yourself should be escorted by a gentleman such as myself."

"Boy, he was so gallant."

"We were in love instantly. We danced until dawn. We've been dancing ever since. Fifty years of marriage, four children and eleven grandchildren."

What a life!

"I'm going to miss Joe. But I believe we'll be together again someday. In fact, I'm sure of it."

"I am so sorry for your loss, Eleanor. It must be even more difficult to lose Joe on the special day."

"My dear," Eleanor said with a big smile, "this is the anniversary of the day we met. "Joe and I met on Valentine's Day 1941!"

NINETEEN

He Is Not Leaving

Dispatcher call: "Patient fell. Wife can't get her husband to respond. Needing a visit."

I had been sleeping since midnight on this cold January night. The temperature outside was near zero. The winds were blowing at thirty miles an hour with gusts above fifty. I was dreading going out to my car.

But as always, I got moving.

I quickly washed my face and dressed. Heavy underwear and thick wool socks. The new heavy coat was going to be tested tonight.

I ran to my car, started the engine, and headed back inside until the car heater warmed the interior. It only took a few minutes. Thank goodness for modern technology!

No traffic tonight. The drive to the home of the patient only took twenty minutes. As I approached the house, 302 Wilton Drive, I could barely see the numbers on the door. GPS said I arrived; I hoped it was correct. The only sign of life was a dim light shining through the front window, toward the right. There was a back door visible to me as I drove a little closer with my car.

Suddenly, I saw a figure inside the glass door. Mrs. Goldstine was waving me inside. I quickly grabbed my nurse bag and walked up toward the door.

"Hi, I'm Pepper, the nurse."

"Thank you. I'm Mrs. Goldstine. Please hurry."

We both rushed to the living room, and there he was. Mr. Goldstine. Lying flat on the floor.

Mrs. Goldstine explained, "He was going to the bathroom, and he just dropped to the floor. I can't wake him up. Can you help him?"

I knew in an instant that Mr. Goldstine was no longer with us.

No longer among the living.

Mrs. Goldstine was not going to take this well.

Mr. Issac Goldstine was a retired college professor. At age eighty-nine, he was still married to Myrna, his wife of sixty years.

Issac was diagnosed with congestive heart failure more than two years ago. He had been on hospice for almost ten months. The medications he was prescribed became less and less effective due to his worsening condition and the progression of his disease. He had difficulty breathing all the time despite taking diuretics to remove excess fluid around his lungs and breathing treatments to rescue him when he was in respiratory distress. Liquid morphine and lorazepam were being administered to Issac by Myrna around the clock for symptom relief.

I knelt down beside my patient and felt for his pulse.

There was none.

No breaths, no movement at all.

Time of death: 3:25 a.m.

I looked up at Myrna and softly stated, "I'm so sorry. Issac has passed away."

His beloved wife started to sob and tremble in her chair. I stood to console her.

"Is there anyone I can call for you, Mrs. Goldstine?" I inquired.

"No," she answered. "We have each other. It's been that way for a very long time."

The first order of business was to get Issac off the floor. He was a tall man and looked to weigh over two hundred pounds. I called 911 and requested a lift and assist. This is a courtesy service that some local paramedics provide to patients at home when they fall and cannot get back up on their own.

The paramedics arrived in record time and placed Issac in his bed. Once there, I began my postmortem care. I asked Myrna to choose some clothes for Issac, and I began washing him with warm water and soap. I carefully dressed him after his bath and asked Myrna if I could assist her with calling the funeral home.

"No, thank you," was her immediate answer. "I read somewhere that I can keep Issac here for as long as I want. You can go home now, and I will call the undertaker when I'm ready."

This was the first time I heard that from a caregiver. I wasn't sure how to handle this situation. Normally, our organization does not interfere with the arrangements for burial. Once we pronounce the patient, we leave the loved ones to take care of the final arrangements.

In this case, it appeared Myrna was not going to allow Issac to leave the house.

At least not in the normal amount of time.

As I was thinking about how to handle the situation, I looked around the room and noticed a few things.

The bedroom where Issac was now resting was a tiny bedroom with limited furniture. He was lying in a double bed that was probably purchased when they first married. The dressers, nightstands, lamps, and armoire all matched the aging headboard. The curtains on the window were a cotton blend with faded white sheers in the center.

There was something very comforting about the room, like it had been blessed with many happy memories.

Myrna fixed what little hair was left on Issac's head. Put his eyeglasses on and said, "Now can you go? I want to be alone with my husband."

I again asked her if she needed me to call the funeral home.

Her reply was the same.

"No, thank you."

I was not going to leave this now-deceased patient without knowing where he would be taken for a final resting place. I began a discussion with Myrna as I usually do after pronouncing a patient.

"How long have you been together?" I started.

Myrna began by thanking me for coming. She then informed me that she and Issac were married a few years ago, and they had no children.

I began doubting Myrna. The story did not match with the one told earlier.

I reminded her that our records show she was married to Issac for a very long time, and they have a son. I also reminded her about the plans she didn't have for a funeral.

Myrna said, "What are you doing here?"

I took a deep breath and told Myrna, "Give me a moment. I want to look at Issac's chart."

I opened my computer and typed Issac's name. The full medical chart populated on the screen. On the side of the screen, there was an alert that read, "Please be aware that the patient's wife has new-onset dementia. Other caregiver information listed in chart."

Listed in the caregiver section was the name of their son, Jacob Goldstine. I dialed the phone number, and the person on the other end said, "Hello?"

I identified myself, "Hi, I am Pepper, the nurse taking care of Issac Goldstine. Is this Jacob?"

"Yes, it is. How can I help you?"

"I'm so sorry to have to tell you, your dad, Issac, has passed away tonight."

There was a minute of silence on the phone, and then Jacob answered.

"Thank you for calling and letting me know. I will be right over. I live just around the corner. How is my mother?"

"She is doing fine right now. I'm not sure she is comprehending what has happened."

"Please tell her I will be there soon."

"I certainly will," I assured Jacob.

It only took Jacob a few minutes to arrive. When he did, his mother seemed distant to him.

"Hi, Mom. It's me, Jacob."

Myrna barely acknowledged her son. She smiled and started to speak.

"My husband is resting and can't leave right now," she told her son. "This nice man over here wants to send Issac away. I will not allow that."

Jacob was very tense, and tears were filling his eyes. He looked at me and said, "She was just diagnosed with dementia a few months ago. Everything seemed to be under control. I was here this afternoon, and she was eating and laughing. Everything was fine."

Everything was not fine. I attempted to explain the possible reasons for Myrna's increased confusion. I explained that the sudden death of a spouse can trigger an acute onset of Alzheimer's disease. Because she was just diagnosed with dementia, it was certainly possible that Issac's sudden passing might have caused her confusion to become much worse almost instantly.

Jacob brought two chairs from the kitchen and set them next to the bed. He sat Myrna in one chair and he in the other. They began to pray together.

After several minutes of prayer and calm emotional support from her son, Myrna agreed to let us call the funeral home for her husband.

TWENTY

Thirty Minutes More

Dispatcher call: "New infusion orders, morphine IV."

I gathered my nursing bag and walked to my car. The weather has changed in recent days. It had been unusually warm compared with most years. Temperatures in the fifties during the day and no colder than thirty-five degrees at night.

Tonight was freezing! Twenty-two degrees and winds blowing at thirty miles per hour.

I started the engine and turned the heater on high. I was warmed and ready to go in a matter of minutes. I tuned the radio to my favorite talk station to catch up on the latest news and political gossip. The roads were deserted. I would get to my destination quickly.

I arrived at 2352 Asher Lane, a large mansion that was situated two hundred yards off the road. There was a beautifully landscaped front lawn with a wraparound driveway made from tan pavers. I drove in and parked next to a vintage 350SL Mercedes. Light-blue. I turned my coat collar up to help me brace the cold winds and headed up the front steps to the large set of double doors made of oak. I rang the doorbell.

The door opened, and I was greeted by an attractive middle-aged Hispanic-looking woman.

"Hi, I'm the nurse from hospice, Pepper."

"Hello, I'm Maria, Isabella's daughter. Please come in."

"Thank you," I quickly replied, grateful to come into the warm house and out of the bitter cold.

Isabella was a ninety-year-old Puerto Rican woman who was originally from San Juan. She was forced to move here after her home was destroyed in Hurricane Maria in 2017. She was on dialysis three days a week. She, along with thousands of other patients, were desperate for treatment due to the electricity outages across the entire area. Maria had her mother flown to New Jersey to live with her. Soon after she arrived, Isabella went into heart failure. Medications to remove fluid from around her heart and to control her blood pressure were effective for several months, but her condition had worsened; and now Isabella was having difficulty breathing.

Maria had been administering liquid morphine, 10 milligrams every two hours, to help her mother breathe. In this situation, our organization places the patient on an infusion to make the administration of the morphine more even over time and to allow the caregiver to have quality time with their loved ones and not be overwhelmed with the clinical aspects of care.

As I entered the room, I was struck by the scent of lavender. There were three candles spaced evenly around the room, burning brightly. This particular scent has a calming effect. It was also a favorite of my mother's. I also noticed several crucifixes on the walls and one placed directly over the headboard. There was even a portrait of Jesus sitting on the nightstand next to the patient.

As I approached my patient, I could see she was still struggling to breathe, despite her current schedule of medications. I immediately administered an additional dose of morphine and began preparations to start the infusion.

As I was setting up for the infusion, Isabella grabbed my wrist and locked her beautiful blue eyes on mine. She began muttering words I did not understand. I looked over at Maria for help with interpreting. Maria explained to me what her mother was speaking in Spanish.

"My mother is very fearful that starting her on an infusion of morphine will cause her to die sooner. She is asking to have thirty minutes more to talk to me alone."

"I will wait for as long as you need," I replied.

I looked over at Isabella, smiled, nodded in agreement and left mother and daughter alone.

While they had their quality time together, I sat with Jose, Maria's husband. He shared the story of how he met Maria. She was working as a waitress in a local coffee shop where he would have lunch on his break from his job on a construction site.

It was love at first sight!

He smiled as he remembered how quickly they were married after dating for only four months. They spent their honeymoon in San Juan to be close to Isabella. Soon, Maria was pregnant with little Jose.

Thirty minutes went by quickly, and Maria appeared in front of Jose and me.

"Mom is ready for her infusion."

"I'll go in and get things started," I said.

As I set up the supplies to start the IV, I noticed Isabella's breathing had changed. Her breaths were shallow, and she now had periods of apnea. Some patients experience a short time, maybe a second or two, when breathing stops and begins again.

I placed a tiny needle into the fatty area on the back of her right upper arm and secured it in place with a clear dressing. I then connected the tubing from the infusion pump to the site with the needle I placed. I started the pump.

Isabella was now having 3 milligrams of morphine being delivered into her body every hour.

I gathered the excess supplies and debris to place in the trash. I covered my patient with a warm blanket and said goodbye to Maria and Jose.

On the drive home, I received a phone call from my dispatcher. "Isabella has passed away. Please return to pronounce the patient."

Jose met me at the door and led me back to the bedroom where Isabella was being taken care of.

Maria was in the bed with her mother, her face soaked with tears. She immediately stood up and rushed over to me. Without hesitation, I offered a consoling embrace.

"Thank you so much for caring for my mother," Maria whispered.

"You are welcome," was my reply.

Within minutes, there were two dozen friends and relatives entering the home. Some brought coffee and donuts; others brought sandwiches and soda.

Time of death: 10:15 p.m.

When I requested the warm water, Maria informed me that during her private talk with Isabella, her mother had specific requests. First, and most important, Isabella asked Maria to be the person to prepare her for the funeral home.

"Is that okay with you?" Maria asked.

I nodded in agreement. "I will honor any wishes your mom has made."

Isabella was a devout Catholic. Her wishes included other common practices, such as visitation at the funeral home and traditional full mass at the church.

Hispanic culture is bold, colorful, and vibrant. An impromptu visitation began immediately after I pronounced Isabella and Maria prepared her body. Family members brought pan dulce and pastelitos to the house. Beautiful flowers delivered and candles lit for Isabella. Family members started to prepare for novenarios, nine consecutive days of prayer following the funeral to ensure eternal rest for their loved one. Music from mariachi began playing, and Maria's home was turned into a celebration.

The mourning will come later.

For now, we celebrate Isabella.

"Mom planned all of this in those last thirty minutes. Of course, we said our goodbyes, but Mom really wanted to make sure I honored all of her requests."

I told Maria that I believe they were both lucky to have had such a beautiful time together just before Isabella passed away.

Maria walked me to the door as I was leaving.

"Thank you so much for everything. Mom also instructed me to thank you. She said to tell you that you are an angel sent from God."

We hugged one more time, and I walked to my car, tears streaming down my face.

It is an honor and privilege to care for my patients. They are the angels as they leave us to go to heaven.

TWENTY-ONE

Not Ready Yet

My favorite birthday celebration was my tenth. The year was 1969.

September 19.

I was in the fifth grade, St. Joseph Catholic School in New Jersey. There were only twenty-five students in my homeroom. I invited every classmate to my special day.

Everyone showed up with great presents. No present could top the one that came from my father.

A Seeburg jukebox!

I loved to dance and sing along with each 45 rpm record as they played after they were selected. Simon and Garfunkel's "Mrs. Robinson." Gary Lewis's "Save Your Heart for Me." The Beatles' "Here Comes the Sun." The Four Seasons' "Working My Way Back to You." And many more.

Music helps create emotional conditions. It makes you calm, happy, and serene. Music touches our soul. Music enables us to express ourselves what we cannot verbally express at times. It has long been considered to be a natural way to ease emotional pain. Scientists are convinced that humans are hardwired to respond to music. As you have read in this book, music is essential to my emotional and spiritual well-being as I navigate to and from sad, anxious, and life-changing events. Often, families play the patient's favorite music as they pass on to another world, or immediately after. My mother listened to Broadway musicals, opera, and some contemporary artists. I believe the music kept her calm during the storm known as cancer.

Dispatcher call: "Mr. Simmons is in respiratory distress, daughter is very emotional, needs visit now."

I grabbed my nursing bag and walked to my car. It was a very mild day in March. Temperature in the midseventies, and a beautiful cloudless sky. Traffic was heavy. Everyone was getting out of the house. Driving to the mall, a park, or even the beach.

I turned my car onto Grove Street and parked on the curb in front of number 303. The front lawn was a mess. Patches of dead grass and weeds were everywhere. An old broken bike with one wheel blocked the sidewalk as I made my way to the front door. Before I could knock on the storm door, a young woman appeared on the other side of the dirty glass. She immediately opened the door to let me inside.

"Hi, I'm Pepper from hospice," I introduced myself.

The young woman was an emotional mess. She obviously had been crying. Her face stained with dried tears. Her hair was tied in a rubber band and set to the side. Her voice was trembling as she started telling me what was happening with her father.

As I walked into the living room, I recognized the foul odor of old kitty litter that needs cleaning. There were multiple worn toys and dirty stuffed animals strewn over worn-out furniture that apparently was clawed at by the same cats who did their business in that box.

"These are my kids, Luke and Maria," the woman stammered.

"Daddy was having a good day," she began. "He woke at 8:00 a.m. and ate a small breakfast. We talked for a little while, and I started my daily routine. Feeding the children and getting them ready for school. The bus is always early."

"Are you Suze?"

"Yes, I am."

Mr. Simmons, aged ninety-four, had been dying of complications of mesothelioma. He had been in the United States Navy during World War II. After honorably serving his country, Mr. Simmons landed a decent job in the shipyards. The fact that he had had such a long life is remarkable. A few months ago, he began feeling breathless and short of breath. He had a CT scan of the chest along with some blood work.

His physician gave him the bad news in person.

Mr. Simmons was terminal!

There were not many options for our veteran. So with the advice of his physician, he signed on to hospice. Until today, our patient had had adequate symptom management using supplemental oxygen and liquid morphine.

As soon as I walked through the doorway leading to Mr. Simmons, I immediately saw him in his hospital bed. He was gray and very still. His mouth was open; lips were motionless. His chest was not rising up and down.

Mr. Simmons appeared to have departed from us.

I walked over and bent over the side rails to assess my patient closer. I placed my hand on his eyelid to check his pupils. At that instant, Mr. Simmon's right hand swiftly rose, and I was pushed away.

"What are you doing?" he shouted in a weak voice.

"I am sorry to disturb you," was my reply.

Mr. Simmons was not dead!

Suze started sobbing, "Daddy, you are still here. I love you."

"Of course I'm still here. I'm not ready to leave yet."

I began my assessment on my patient. Temperature 98.0, heart rate 62 and weak, blood pressure 94/50, and respiration only 8 per minute with periods of apnea.

My patient was hanging on, just barely.

Mr. Simmons quickly fell back into a deep sleep. Suze had been administering 20 milligrams of liquid morphine every hour to control her father's shortness of breath.

As I was finishing my assessment, I began to notice my surroundings. The room where my patient was being cared for was very unique. The floor was a combination of black and white tiles resembling a chess board. The windowsill was at least seven feet long and two feet deep. It was packed with several Lionel Trains. Then, I looked past Mr. Simmons and could not believe my eyes. All along, the twenty-foot-long wall was his prized collection.

Six vintage jukeboxes!

He had a Seeburg model "Trash Can," a 1950 all-glass top model, and a 1948 wall box classic, the kind we used to see in a diner, all loaded with everyone's favorite 45s.

My heart was filled with such memories.

I told Suze about my tenth birthday and my special gift. It seemed to offer comfort to her, and I observed as she began breathing a little easier and managed a smile.

I instructed her to continue administering the morphine as needed and to call the hospice answering service with any concerns. I told Suze that I was working on call around the clock and would be very willing to come back out for her father. Suze and I hugged, and I was on my way.

Dispatcher call: "Mr. Simmons has passed away. Please pronounce."

It had only been a few days since I first met Mr. Simmons. I remembered those jukeboxes in his room next to his bed. How comforting it was for him as he was preparing for his death. I also remembered my jukebox. I use music as a source of comfort, inspiration, and strength as I navigate through the tasks I perform for my patients and their families.

I arrived at the house and rushed inside to Suze. I needed to be totally sure our patient had passed away. This time, no one met me at the door. I knocked and waited to enter.

"Come in," Suze said as she opened the door.

"Hello again, may I go right back?"

"Of course."

This time, things looked very different. My patient was motionless, and his eyes were open and completely dilated. His skin color was sallow yellow.

Mr. Simmons was gone.

Passed away.

In heaven with many others.

WARM WATER

I proceeded to perform my usual assessment for the benefit of Suze. No respirations, no pulse, no blood pressure.

"I'm sorry. He is gone this time."

Time of death: 5:55 p.m.

Suze was remarkably calm. She shed a couple of tears, offered half a smile, and began talking about her beloved father.

As she talked, I retrieved the basin from the bathroom closet and filled it with warm water so I could bathe Mr. Simmons.

"Dad was always supportive of my decisions in life. He came to live with me after my husband ran off with another woman. If it wasn't for him, I would have lost my home and kids. Now, I'm not sure what I'll be able to do," she said while sobbing.

I explained that our social worker might be able to help her with that. Next question for Suze was if she needed assistance with funeral arrangements or spiritual support. Her answer took me by surprise.

"I don't need any help. Dad was an atheist and raised me to be atheist as well."

As a hospice nurse, I am not only responsible for the medical care of my patients but the spiritual as well. This posed a challenge for me because I had never encountered this situation before. I am usually able to offer appropriate support using my personal knowledge of many religions. They include Catholic, Protestant, Lutheran, Baptist, Presbyterian, and patients of the Jewish faiths. I have cared for patients who follow Hinduism, Buddhism, Muslim, and Christian faiths.

Never someone with no faith.

After searching my soul for guidance on how to handle the situation, I remembered my role as the hospice nurse. My role is to manage pain and other symptoms, provide support to patients and families, and assist in the process of death with dignity. Now that Mr. Simmons was pronounced, I turned my attention to Suze.

I began this new conversation by asking her what her beliefs were in regard to the afterlife. Suze's answer was simple and direct.

"We do not believe in the afterlife of any God or heaven. We do believe that our physical energy remains here on earth. It is just transferred to another form. It sounds complicated to most people, and I understand that. I respect the beliefs of others and expect the same in return."

I answered just as simply and directly, "I understand."

While I have consoled many patients' families of many different faiths, one thing remains constant. People need to grieve. Our responsibility is to assist and encourage survivors of loss to begin the process. Grief is at the very heart of being human. Rituals that facilitate the process of grief have long been a part of the religions of the world. Whether wearing black or a special piece of clothing, overt crying, or beating one's breast, many religions encourage rituals to trigger the grieving process.

It seems people without faith may have difficulty with that process.

I respect whatever someone believes. My responsibility is to offer emotional support and reassurance, regardless of what a grieving family believes or does not believe.

"I am so sorry for your loss. If you need anything, please don't hesitate to reach out to us. We will contact you from time to time," I explained.

Suze smiled and said, "If I did believe in such things, then you must be an angel!"

TWENTY-TWO

If These Walls Could Talk

Dispatcher call: "Patient has passed away. Please pronounce."

When I read the address of the patient, I could not believe my eyes. It was the house where I spent the better part of the first ten years of my life. A place I hadn't seen in more than fifty years.

I grabbed my nursing bag and ran to my car with nervous excitement. I started the engine, turned on the radio, and began my trip.

The old homestead was only five miles from where I live now. The journey to this pronouncement seemed to take forever. There was very little traffic due to curfews put in place during the COVID-19 pandemic.

Very anxious times.

George, an eighty-eight-year-old Italian Catholic man, had been suffering from COPD for many years. He had also been dependent on continuous oxygen for the past several months. George had been admitted to the local hospital at least six times in the past year. He would receive breathing treatments and an antibiotic and be discharged home. Only to be right back to the emergency room in a matter of weeks. George had become frustrated with this cycle and decided to stop going to the hospital and sign on to hospice.

That was one month ago.

As I parked in front of the house, a flood of memories came into my head. The small front lawn, the front porch. It was almost spooky and yet comfortable. Because of the pandemic, I was required to wear protective equipment to help prevent the spread of this deadly virus. I put on a plastic gown, goggles, mask, and gloves. I walked up the two steps and knocked on the door.

Just then, I remembered walking through that same threshold five decades ago as I was going to school. Cold, hot, rain, or shine, or after a snowfall, my two older siblings and I walked to school.

A young woman answered my knock.

"Hi, I'm Pepper, from hospice," I stated.

"Hello, I'm Karen. My grandfather is in the back room."

I was speechless. The house looked exactly the way I remembered it after all these years. The stairs to the second floor were right there as I walked in. The dining room was to the right, and the living room was farther back on the same side.

That was where George was.

Everything seemed so much smaller than I remembered.

I immediately checked my patient. No pulse, no respirations. It was all so familiar and sad as always. George was gone. I turned around to face Karen and two other young ladies, who turned out to be her sisters, Gerty and Joanne.

"I'm so sorry for your loss."

"Thank you, Pepper. We are going to miss Grandpa," she said with tears rolling down her cheeks.

Time of death: 8:50 p.m.

I took the basin next to George's bed and went into the kitchen to fill it with warm water.

"Do you have arrangements made with a funeral home?"

"Yes, should I call them now?" Karen asked.

"Yes, tell them that George was pronounced and he is ready to go."

I finished washing my patient and dressed him in the clothes that Joanne brought me.

Karen commented on how peaceful her grandfather looked. She seemed very comforted.

I asked, "Did George live here with you?"

"Actually, this is George's house," she said. "My sisters and I live here with him. It worked out great because we were able to care for him."

"That's so nice you could do that for him. You guys all seem so close," I replied.

"We are. Grandpa is giving the house to us now. He and Grandma lived here their entire marriage that lasted forty-eight years. Grandma died less than two years ago from heart failure. Grandpa was never the same after that."

"Wow, that is very interesting. I need to tell you something," I said excitedly. "I lived in this house until I was ten years old. Right before your grandparents moved here."

"Are you serious?" she replied.

"Yes. My family lived here for several years during the decade of the sixties. By the time we moved out, we were a family of seven. Mom, Dad, me, and my older brother, along with three sisters. I remember so much now that I'm here talking to you. The kitchen seemed so much larger back then."

"Did you ever run in and out of the rooms while playing tag down here?"

"We had to behave due to so many people. Most of the time was playing outside with siblings and cousins. At the time, there were around ten of us, including myself, my older brother, and older sister. It felt like we were outside from sunup until sundown," I said while smiling.

Karen started to laugh. "We had almost the same rules growing up. We lived here with our grandparents all of our childhood. Both of our parents died in a car accident in 1957. They were wonderful. We had many happy times."

"Can I ask for a special favor?" I asked. "May I take a look upstairs?"

"Sure, go ahead," she agreed very graciously.

As I ascended up the stairs, I thought back to all those years when I used to walk up those same steps as a young boy. Once at the top, I saw the old bathroom. A quick right into what used to be Mom and Dad's bedroom. And then, there at the back of the house was my old bedroom. It still looked the same. In fact, all of the current furniture was in the same position as when I slept in it with my brother.

It was as if I never left.

As I looked out the bedroom window into the dark night, I could make out the apple tree under the moonlit sky. I also remembered there was a cherry tree at the far end of the backyard.

Memory after memory came through one after the other.

I came back down the stairs and offered my condolences once again. I had to inform the girls about the strict guidelines in place because of the pandemic. The state would not be allowing gatherings of more than ten people. This meant that a viewing at the funeral home would be out of the question. Social distancing was already in place, and there would certainly be limits at the cemetery. The ability to grieve is an important step in being able to move on with our lives after losing a loved one through death. This was being made nearly impossible by this disease. Spiritual support is a very special task performed by the hospice team. It was my responsibility at that moment.

"I read that George was Catholic. Considering that your time with him might be very limited after he leaves here, would you like to pray? I'm Catholic as well."

All three girls agreed, and I followed their lead. We recited the Our Father and several Hail Marys.

It was beautiful.

Karen thanked me and told me that the coincidence of me being the person to pronounce their beloved grandpa was a blessing. She was also comforted by the shared memories in that house.

As I made my exit and looked at the street from the porch, I had one more pleasant memory. When we were living there, we had an Uncle Jack who worked at the Tastykake plant in Philadelphia. Several times a year, he would visit and bring each child their favorite cake. Mine were mini powdered donuts.

I stopped at a local convenience store on the way home and purchased a pack!

EPILOGUE

My career as a hospice nurse affords me the honor and privilege to care for people at a time when they may be at their most vulnerable. A time of anxiety and fear. A time of reflection and reconciliation. A time of peace and resolve. The patients are my first priority. Their needs are attended to first. It is the very sad understanding and expectation that every patient that signs on to hospice, with a few exceptions, is going to die under our care. It is my job to alleviate the pain, shortness of breath, and anxiety of the dear souls. My job is to allow them to die with dignity. I give them full control to make the decisions about their care. They are, after all, the ones who must summon the courage to face their own mortality. It is being witness to that courage, strength, and resolve that inspires me to continue my work. I am very fortunate to work for an organization that effectively utilizes the teamwork paradigm. They encourage this concept by continually leading by example and by always being available with support when called upon. Each of us in a team and as part of the organization plays a vital role in caring for our patients and families. We likewise play a vital role in supporting other members of the team and organization to achieve those same goals.

Each pronouncement I perform is a chance for me to connect with other human beings. To comfort the families in those moments of sadness and loss. As illustrated throughout this book, all people—regardless of race, gender, or religion—feel that sense of loss and sadness. By allowing those families to talk and reminisce about their recently departed, they are able to begin the grieving process. At the same time, I recognize the parallel to my own life, and it becomes cathartic for me as well.

PEPPER CAPPUCCIO

What a beautiful gift to offer one another!

> Perhaps they are not stars, but rather openings in heaven where the love of our lost ones pours through and shines down upon us to let us know they are happy. (Eskimo proverb)

ABOUT THE AUTHOR

The author of Warm Water has been a Hospice Nurse for more than ten years. In that period of time, he has had the honor and privilege to assist hundreds of patients through the dying process as well as perform the tasks associated with a patient at, or just after they pass away. An intimate bond is formed almost immediately between the patient. their caregivers, and the author.

The author, being Catholic, has a strong faith and belief in the principles of caring for others, and is well rewarded spiritually by such acts. He became a registered nurse more than fifteen years ago, however, it was not until he experienced the death of his own mother that he realized his true calling. Hospice Nursing is what brings him joy and satisfaction.

The author is naturally compassionate and is acutely aware of the challenges faced by the caregivers as they face the loss of their dearly departed. The author is instantly able to connect the similarities of each patient/family as it relates to his own life's experiences.

A catharsis is realized by both the author and the caregivers every time someone passes on.

CPSIA information can be obtained
at www.ICGtesting.com
Printed in the USA
BVHW031735090321
602112BV00008B/703